Chronicles of Rhenania
-0-
Living with the Lion and the Unicorn
-0-
Conflict as never before

Robin Scutarius

Copyright © 2017
All rights reserved.
ISBN-10: 1981110909
ISBN-13: 978-1981110902

DEDICATION

To Josef Holzbacher
1867 - 1943
A kind and loving man
whose family was his greatest treasure

CONTENTS

Chronicles of Rhenania
Chapter 1: "Where do we come from?"
Chapter 2: The chronicle of Heinrich Paul 1746 - 1813
Chapter 3: The chronicle of Susanna (Paul) Steinbrecher 1776 - 1831
Chapter 4: How Kreuznach found favour and the Chronicle of Katharina (Steinbrecher) Maurer 1805 - 1883
Chapter 5: The chronicle of Jacob Steinbrecher 1807 - 1855
Chapter 6: Kirn, the town known as the place of leather, stone and beer
Chapter 7: The chronicle of Georg Valentin Holzbacher 1833 - 1919 Part one

Living with the Lion and the Unicorn
Chapter 8: The Emigrants and Georg Valentin Holzbacher 1833 - 1919 Part two
Chapter 9: Elise tells her story
Chapter 10: Celebration and thanksgiving

Conflict as never before
Chapter 11: How so few can destroy so many
Chapter 12: Peace in their time?

6

Chronicles of Rhenania

CHAPTER ONE

"WHERE DO WE COME FROM?"

Louise sat at the drawing room window, looking out on the wintry street in north London. The morning fog had cleared to greet a pale sun, highlighting the terrace of town houses on the other side of the road. Louise and her family had lived here for nearly nine years now and were on friendly terms with their neighbours. A movement caught her eye, and Louise looked further up to the end of terrace house where the doctor lived. As she watched, the horse and carriage came round from the side of the house, driven by the doctor himself. If there was an emergency, he would be urging on his horse but, this time, he turned into the street and pulled up by the front gate. His wife came out from the front door, with its stained glass panel, descended the front steps and down the black and white tiled path. As she turned from closing the gate, her husband helped her up into the carriage. She was a midwife and had delivered most of the babies in the street, including Louise's brother and sister, but today her easy manner told there was no baby arriving at that moment.

As the couple drove off and there was nothing more to be seen, Louise turned back to her thoughts. She was a happy child and loved her life. She liked her school friends, some of whom - like herself - were from other countries. She felt that the mix of English and European was enriching, and she enjoyed listening to her young friends telling of different customs they had at home. Her own parents, Carl and Elise, had left their homeland of Germany in the early 1880s and come to England where, they had been informed by relatives, they would be able to make a better life. Her father's abilities and diligence had led him to the position of chief clerk in a small company importing essential oils from Europe and the Middle East. Once married, Louise's parents had been able to rent a terraced house with enough room for an expanding family. It was also near to the developing network of railways both over- and underground which brought her father swiftly to his work in the City of London, and home again. With the commerce increasing and room at home, Carl suggested to his youngest brother Josef that he also should join him and Elise. With their parents both no longer alive and Josef's training in Germany finished, it seemed like the best idea. Very soon Louise was born, followed three years later by a brother Charlie. Another brother was born some four years afterwards and lost in infancy. Now, just after her tenth birthday, the family had joyfully welcomed another baby girl Elisabeth, to be called Elsa.

Louise left her window seat and, grabbing a big cushion, went to sit on the floor beside her Uncle Josef, who was reading a book in front of the brightly burning fire. Her brother Charlie was playing with some carved wooden farm animals. They could hear the new baby crying in the room above, then a sudden silence - and they guessed it was feeding time.

"Uncle Josef" murmured Louise. "Louise" he replied. He looked up from his book and considered his young niece. "What is troubling you, my precious?"

"Uncle Josef, where do we come from?" Louise looked up hopefully, and Charlie stopped playing with his animals. He had wondered about that too, so he pottered over to sit on the floor by his big sister.

Josef put down his book and rose to fetch a large atlas from the bookshelf. He sat down on the rug by the children and opened the book. After flicking through a few pages he found the map he wanted.

"Come and sit each side of me, children" he said. "Here, do you see, this area is commonly known as Rhenania. It is to the west of this long wide river called the Rhine, flowing from Switzerland in the south along hundreds of miles northwards to Holland where it flows into the North Sea". Josef pointed to a place on the map saying

"Rhenania is this region with France to the south-west, Belgium to the west and, beyond Cologne, to the north are the low countries known as the Netherlands".

"I have heard Papa and Mama talking about Kirn and Kreuznach. Where are those places?" asked Charlie.

Josef traced a blue line on the map. "This is the river Rhine and, if you find the riverside town of Bingen, you will notice another smaller river called the Nahe.. See it? And if we go slightly up, or north-west, we come to the town of Bad Kreuznach and, following on a little, we see another little town called Kirn. Your Mama comes from Kirn and, although we were not born there, your Papa and I lived in Kreuznach until each of us left in turn to come to England. We have family and friends in both places but feel that this is now our home".

"Uncle Valentine says that, although he will only ever be a German, home is where you make it" said Louise.

"Uncle Valentine …. ah yes" said Josef thoughtfully. "Well, you can ask him his story another time but I think could be a bit confusing for you right now. But let me tell you about the first of our ancestors whose story I learnt some time ago. His name is Heinrich Paul, and he was your great-great-… great-grandfather!"

"Oooh he would be very very old now"!

Josef smiled. "Indeed. He would be almost one hundred and fifty years old! But come, snuggle up near the fire and I will tell you about him".

CHAPTER TWO

THE CHRONICLE OF HEINRICH PAUL 1746 - 1813

The years of learning and labour

The story of Heinrich Paul is a simple one of its time. Still almost a baby, Heinrich became an orphan when both his parents died within weeks of each other. His godfather Johann Lotz took him into the care of his family. Mr. Lotz was a hosier, or maker of socks and stockings and even, on occasion when requested specially, of fine underwear. However, this did not make a great deal of money, and so it was necessary to ask for help from the town magistrate towards the education of young Heinrich.

Heinrich was an obedient child, eager to please, and learnt his lessons well. The region was subjected to continual changes of administration when the French invaded and reigned, until the Prussians counter-invaded and imposed German administration. As all children in those towns and villages, Heinrich also learned to speak and write both German and French. It was how the population adapted to whoever was in command. Babies born under French rule were given French names such as Jean or Sophie which then, under German rule, could easily be germanicised as Johann and Sophia.

When Heinrich had finished his basic education at the age of thirteen, his guardians decided he should be a painter-decorator as his father had been before him. To familiarise him with the essence of such work, Heinrich was sent to work with the local painter-decorator. It soon became apparent that he was well suited to this profession and, on recommendation of his employer, his guardians arranged for him to go to Frankfurt to be apprenticed to a master craftsman well known for his excellent work in the art of specialist decorating. At fourteen it was quite usual, and even necessary, for boys to become apprentices to learn a trade or craft for their future. So Heinrich took his leave of his godfather Lotz and the only family he had known, then shouldered his backpack containing his few clothes, a precious pair of shoes, and letters of recommendation for his new master. It was a bright spring morning when he set out through the town gate and up in to the hills. His young friends had accompanied him to the top of the first hill where they took leave of him. He turned to look one last time at the familiar little town - how long would it be until he saw it again? The boys waved as he strode out, barefoot, until he disappeared behind the trees. At first he came close to tears as he felt the loneliness, but then he thought of all the new things he would see and learn, and the momentary sadness passed.

Heinrich knew it would take him two days to get to Frankfurt, and the first day's walk would take him to a small town called Friedberg, where his godfather had acquaintances who would take him in for the night. They welcomed him with a hot evening meal, warm water to wash himself, and a straw mattress in the eaves to rest his tired legs and sleep. They had also found a place for him on a cart leaving the next day which would take him near to Frankfurt. This meant he could be at the city gates well ahead of their closing by the French troops occupying Frankfurt for the past year. Everything went as planned, and he was grateful for the ride in the cart. As he approached the city on foot, he encountered many horse riders and carriages who were leaving after the Easter fair. Heinrich had never seen so many different vehicles, some of which carried strange animals such as bears, monkeys and wild beasts in cages.

Finally he reached the Friedberg gate where the French guards inspected his papers. Thanks to the diligence of his godfather, this presented no problem and he was allowed entry into the city. He marvelled at the fortified city walls, the tall townhouses, the finely dressed people and the splendid carriages. He was less impressed by the shabby French soldiers noisily roaming the streets. After enquiring the way to his new master's house, Heinrich went through a high archway into the courtyard which was to become very familiar. The building, dwelling house and workshop, were much bigger than he had been used to. He could see a wealth of equipment and materials in all corners of the yard and workshop.

A young man working in the yard took him to the master, and he explained his presence and presented the letters of recommendation.

Thus Heinrich began the next seven years encompassing his apprenticeship and the bachelor examination which, if successfully completed, led to acceptance into the guild of honourable painter-decorators. This in turn led to work of different kinds to gain experience. Such work was usually in churches or official buildings, but also the fine homes of the wealthy merchants and businessmen - not to mention the grand houses of aristocrats. Heinrich was found to have talents in specialist arts - painting wooden columns, plinths and even boards to simulate marble, applying special varnishes on plain wood to simulate exotic woods, and the application of gold leaf to wood or plaster. He was popular with his colleagues and employers, and he generally enjoyed his life as a young adult. In his spare time he would join friends singing and making music in their homes or in the different church groups very prevalent at the time. Heinrich had a good singing voice, and he learnt to play one or two instruments over time.

It was at one of these musical evenings that he met a young lady named Margarethe Treiber who had come from Kreuznach on a visit to relatives in Frankfurt. Both young people had keen minds and exchanged many thoughts and ideas. After some time it became clear to both of them that they had fallen in love. The time came when Margarethe had to leave Frankfurt and return home. However, Heinrich could not declare the intentions he nurtured - he was doing well but felt he was not yet in a position to offer marriage to the person he treasured above all others. So Margarethe left with hope in her heart and the promise from Heinrich that he would visit her in Kreuznach as soon as he possibly could. But it proved to quite a long wait without the news she so longed for.

What Margarethe did not know at that time was that Heinrich had become a master painter-decorator and had subsequently been asked to decorate the whole interior of a church in Bretzenheim. Once he received the substantial payment for this huge task, which had taken many months to complete, he felt the time had come for him to ask for Margarethe's hand in wedlock. What he in turn did not know was that he was almost too late - Margarethe's parents were asking her to agree to marriage with the most recent in a line of suitors from Kreuznach, all of whom were good and suitable men but whom she continually turned down. When she was finally giving up all hope of seeing him again, Heinrich arrived with a spring in his step. He had kept his promise as she always knew in her heart that he would. The joy of both young people was plain to see and, when Heinrich asked Margarethe's father for permission to wed her, it was happiness all round.

Husband, father and citizen

The 1770s saw Heinrich and Margarethe establishing themselves in the community with a growing young family. Over the years they had eight children but only three survived to become adults. Heinrich continued for some time as a painter-decorator but it meant travelling further afield and possibly spending weeks away from home. As a loving young father, and a caring husband especially when the babies did not survive, he decided he could provide for them all in other ways. He found he had a talent for music and for teaching and, combining the two, found increasing demand in highly respected local families. He became great friends with a landowner, one Herr von Recum, who placed great importance on music in the life of his household. Herr von Recum was passionate about musical instruments and gradually collected enough for a small orchestra. Heinrich taught the children, and contributed to arranging chamber music for the musicians invited to play at concerts. He had also acquired a spinet himself and whenever it was needed for a concert, a farmer's wife would carry it to the concert venue on her head.

In 1783 the region suffered extreme winter conditions followed, in the spring of 1784, by terrible floods. Kreuznach was no exception. The river rose and rose, sweeping away anything along its banks. The bridge in the middle of the town was greatly under threat, and the rising waters started invading the apothecary right next to the bridge. Heinrich and others rushed to the building to help the owner move out. Just as they had brought some heavy furniture to safety further up the street, the apothecary crumbled and was washed away. The helpers were safe but the owner was not so lucky - he was drowned by the rushing waters.

In 1792, probably from necessity, Heinrich took employment in a forge some miles from Kreuznach. There was only one child at home - the oldest son having become a merchant in Mannheim and the second studying theology, leaving just one daughter Susanna aged sixteen with the parents. The forge was in the middle of the forest near Birkenfeld and provided them with accommodation in a small house. There was room for their more modest belongings, the most precious being (for Heinrich!) the spinet which took pride of place in the big room where the family cooked, ate and generally spent their time. Heinrich had of course taught Susanna to play the instrument, and the three of them spent many an evening making music together. However, despite the fact that the forge was the only one in the area and thus well used by local people, its isolation in the forest brought some difficult situations.

The region was still under French occupation, which had given rise to an increasing number of robber bands marauding the countryside. One band led by a young man who called himself

Schinderhannes was particularly active in the area surrounding Kreuznach and its neighbours. Inhabitants, including Heinrich and his family, suffered threats, visits, intimidation and theft by this group. Some of them were known locally and had gone to school with the people to whom they were causing trouble. On several occasions letters were pushed through the doors of the owner of the forge, Mr. Stumm, and Heinrich's house, threatening to set them all on fire unless they paid protection money. On the orders of Mr. Stumm, Heinrich took the ransom money to a specified place where the Schinderhannes group was waiting. He handed over the money and was given a security card to protect him from attack by the bands. This card was copied, reproduced and given to several friends, but the demands for money kept on coming. Finally Mr. Stumm promised a substantial reward to those courageous enough to turn in the robbers. Heinrich passed on this information to one of the gang and, in return, received a promise to stop the demands at the forge. Sometime later a young woman playing a fiddle appeared in front of the house. Margarethe opened the window and gave her a piece of her mind on such idle begging and useless vagabond life. Susanna whispered to her mother to be careful because the woman might belong to the band of robbers and, indeed, some time later the news went round that the leader of one group had taken her as his woman.

The Paul family and others like them continued to live in fear of what could happen. In keeping with the custom of the day, Susanna spent much time working on her trousseau for the day she would marry. She had to begin again twice when the entire trousseau was taken by the robbers. One day Schinderhannes himself, together with eleven men from his band, appeared at the door and demanded entry. He called out that nobody would be hurt and that all they required was a warm meal by the fire. Only the women were at home and finally they decided it was better to let the men in. As Margarethe prepared some food, Schinderhannes ordered Susanna to play the spinet. Trembling, she sat down in front of the spinet but emotion caused her to faint. When she came round, Schinderhannes told her that he would spare her this once - but said he knew she played well because he had listened to her outside on several occasions. With its intricate carving, slender black notes and green felt inlay, the spinet could have told many a tale. Later it had to give up its place to a piano and was relegated to the loft where it became host to a large family of mice. Its subsequent fate is unknown!

Schinderhannes was not all bad; he had a soft spot for children. If he found them walking on lonely paths, he would take them on his shoulders near to their destination. Setting them down, he would apologise for letting them continue alone, saying it was too dangerous for him to come further. Sometimes a family would receive the order to prepare a meal for the robbers to be brought to a specific place. They threatened that, if this was not done, they would move into the home. This happened once when three robbers went to a farm for their meal, but the police had been advised and made a timely arrival. Two robbers escaped but one hid up the big kitchen chimney. When the policemen were looking for the culprit, a child shouted out that they would find him in the chimney. The robber refused to come down until the policemen prepared to light the fire. He then came out as he preferred arrest to burning alive! But later a note was nailed to the farm door warning "Educate your children better".

Finally, however, Schinderhannes was caught after he had stolen bedlinen from a market stall. He was taken to prison and, when he came in front of the magistrate, protested that he had not stolen the items but purchased them from the stallholder, a pale young blond lady in delicate health and prone to fainting. Although terrified she was nevertheless called as a witness - she knew the truth would lead to conviction. She was frightened that, if she maintained the accusation of theft, the robber gangs might damage her shop or hurt her husband who travelled around with their goods. But if she agreed with Schinderhannes, then she herself could be accused of perjury. When she was called to appear, her delicate health prevailed and she fainted. When she regained consciousness, the magistrate reassured her that she would not have to take the oath but should simply state whether Schinderhannes had indeed purchased the bedlinen. She replied that he had, and so he was set free. Some time later, when she was alone in her shop, a fine man in a forester's uniform came in, saying he wanted to thank her for the huge favour she had recently done him. She had no doubt it was Schinderhannes - and duly fainted. When she came round, there was no-one there.

Apart from the trials and tribulations due to the outlaws, the population also suffered other effects of the French occupation. French troops were continually moving around the region, and the forge and its hamlet were raided by their soldiers on more than one occasion. Once, when it had seemed that things were more peaceful, Margarethe decided to do some much needed shopping in Kreuznach. Heinrich was working away from home also, but Susanna assured her mother she would be fine on her own. About to return home again Margarethe learnt that a French convoy was coming through, so she took shelter with a friendly shopkeeper; together, through the shop window, they watched the troops march past. Suddenly she saw a soldier carrying what she recognised as some of her bedlinen, and she became very fearful for her daughter. However, on hearing the soldiers marching along the forest road, Susanna had covered her head and shoulders with an old shawl full of holes, to discourage any of the soldiers from taking liberties. Fortunately the men did not bother her but they took all the food and many belongings. Happily Susanna had hidden some of their bread so that, when another soldier entered the house asking for bread, she replied that it had all been taken. When the soldier then tried to kiss her, she ran upstairs but he followed her. She managed to reach the granary and climbed up into the pigeon coops above. She pulled up the ladder, and the soldier could not reach her. She was safe for a while but made lots of noise, shouting for help and making the pigeons fly around. She was in luck because another platoon arrived with an officer in charge. He heard the commotion and got down from his horse. He went into the house but the soldier had gone. He went upstairs and saw Susanna peering down from the pigeon loft. She told him what had happened, and he helped her down. He opened his bag, took out his own bread and gave it to her. Meanwhile the aggressive soldier had been found, tied on the back of a horse and carted off for punishment. The officer posted a guard in front of the house, and this was changed and continued until the convoys had all passed through. When Susanna's parents finally arrived home later, they were mightily relieved to see that no harm had come to their beloved daughter. Unfortunately not all the French occupiers were so kindly, and many were subjected to punishment for very small matters. It was not unheard of that, if a village was unable to pay its "dues" to the French administrators, the leader of the community would be tied by soldiers to the tail of a horse and dragged through the village.

Towards the end of the century, with Napoleon in power and taking over large parts of Europe (either through military conquest or by means of arranged marriages), Rhenania was still occupied by French troops and run by French administration. However, Heinrich was getting too old for the hard physical work of the forge, and so he moved the family back to Kreuznach. He once more became active in teaching, particularly musical education, and Margarethe and Susanna looked after the household. Margarethe's health was deteriorating and sometimes she longed for the fresh air of the countryside, which was something she had loved about living at the forge in the forest. So Heinrich found a small plot of land some way outside of Kreuznach and built her a little summerhouse. He made a small kitchen, a living room and a little "cellar" to keep things fresh. There was a small garden to grow flowers - tulips in the spring and roses in the summer - and also soft fruit and a few vegetables. It was a good place for the family to come for a picnic. Their two sons had established themselves elsewhere, one as a banker and the other went into the clergy. It was whilst visiting the clergyman son that Margarethe finally became very ill and died. She was greatly missed by Susanna and Heinrich.

In 1813, during a typhus epidemic brought to the region by soldiers of Napoleon's Grande Armée returning from Russia, Heinrich was among those affected. He was actually on the road to recovery and, one day, felt well enough to go out hunting (which he loved) with some friends. He managed to get dressed for the battue but, whilst doing so, suffered a relapse and died. With so many victims of the epidemic, there was no space to bury them in separately, and Heinrich was put in a grave with 12 others. He did not live to see the marching through of Bluecher's Prussian army, on its way to Waterloo to contribute to victory over the French. But he did get to enjoy the excellent wine of the region of the very good 1811 vintage!

-0-0-0-0-0-0-0-0-0-0-

"So you see, my dears", said Josef after a pause. "Life was never very peaceful in the part of Germany we come from. Next time I will tell you about the times which Susanna lived in. She was your great-great-grandmother, and a lot went on in her life too. But enough for today! And it is time for tea".

CHAPTER THREE

About a week later the family was enjoying a quiet Sunday afternoon, again with a brightly burning fire. Carl was reading his newspaper, Elise was adding some embroidered decoration to the christening dress for the baby, and Josef was writing a letter. Louise sidled up to her uncle and stood quietly but expectantly at his side. Charlie, as always, was playing with his carved wooden toys on the rug in front of the fire.

"Uncle Josef ..." said Louise tentatively. "Louise ..." he replied smiling at his young niece. Then he put down his pen. "I know what you would like .. and I did promise you".

Louise's parents looked up. "Now what have you promised, Josef?".

"Well," replied Josef. "The children wanted to know about our homeland, and the relatives who lived - and still do live - there. As you know, I am collecting many of the narratives passed on to us, and I thought it would be good to share them with Louise and Charlie while they are still young and interested".

Carl and Elise agreed wholeheartedly. So Josef fetched the map again, this time with the page marked ready for opening.

"You will remember that, in the story so far, Susanna was still living with her parents and that the family moved back to Kreuznach just before the turn of the century. So now, at 23 years old, Susanna would know a new life as a young woman".

THE CHRONICLE OF SUSANNA (PAUL) STEINBRECHER 1776 - 1831

The town was still under French rule but the new Napoleonic administration was clearer perhaps but also more stringent. Nevertheless, Susanna and her parents settled into their new life again and took up with friends and acquaintances, old and new. Now in her early 20s, Susanna was talented in languages and music. In general the people of the region identified more with their Germanic origins and character, although there had been marriages uniting both French and German ancestral heritage which had led to not only tolerance but also affinity between people. However, if most of the local people could read and write German, not all of them could do so in French even if they could understand and use the spoken word. So Susanna's linguistic skills were often called upon, mostly by the local hotel, to translate French newspapers and official gazettes for the information of the townspeople. Her leisure time was spent with other young people whose greatest pleasures were singing and dancing - generally making music of all sorts.

It was at one of these musical evenings that she met Daniel Steinbrecher, a young glazier, and it was instant love at first sight for both! Daniel's family were originally from southern Germany but had been established in Kreuznach since the early 14th century. That was when the first ancestor came to the town to work in the local quarry, cutting stone for build a bridge across the river Nahe. At that time there was nobody local to the area with such expertise, and so Daniel's ancestor had become known as the Steinbrecher, or stone-breaker = mason. He was rewarded with the permission to keep this name, and the family was later awarded its own crest. Daniel and Susanna married in 1800, and it was almost a "society" wedding. The local gazette reported how the bridegroom wore a blue coat with tails almost to the floor, short black trousers, black and white stockings and shoes with buckles. He wore his hair in a beautifully braided plait bound with ribbon. There was less detail about the bride but it did mention that she was dressed in a light green silk dress with a long train and that she wore a large bonnet.

Susanna and Daniel began their married life at the very beginning of the 19th century, and Daniel had a shop selling not just his own glassware but also highly prized mirrors, and he also added porcelain from elsewhere. Their home became a very lively place as their children began to arrive in quite swift succession, and they eventually had fourteen babies, but only seven survived into adulthood - which was about the norm at the time.

Susanna took her children to enjoy the warmer weather at her mother's summerhouse, and they all enjoyed the fresh air, fruit and vegetables. If it became very hot, they took a picnic and spent the day at a large pond nearby where they could bathe and splash to their heart's content. Mother Margarethe died in 1805, but Susanna took the children there for many years. The family also continued to grow their food there which proved invaluable on occasion, and their small garden was better placed than many when there was bad weather.

During these first years of the century, and especially after the west bank of the Rhine was annexed by the French First Republic in 1801, the Steinbrecher family as all others in the town were obliged to accept lodgers. These were mainly Spanish prisoners of war in long coats, who had been roughly treated by the French and were in very poor health. They were poor fellows, mainly used in building work and other menial jobs for the soldiers. When the French wanted wider streets to accommodate the transport of troops and equipment, the Spanish prisoners were used to simply demolish what stood in their way. However, the Spaniards were generally treated fairly by the population housing them, and some of them became citizens of the town when French occupation ceased. In the autumn of 1804 Napoleon himself visited Kreuznach on two occasions. The saltworks were recognised as being valuable, and in 1808 Napoleon gifted them to his favourite sister Pauline. In 1812 the French army conscripted local men to fight alongside them in the Russian campaign. These men were in a terrible state when they returned to Kreuznach, bringing typhus with them which then caused an epidemic - in which Susanna's father Heinrich died. The following year the Prussian army under General Bluecher joined in the battle of Waterloo, and soon Napoleon's hold over Europe was brought to an end.

After the demise of Napoleon the people of Kreuznach awaited the arrival of the Prussians with much apprehension. The new rulers were known to be more reserved, in the manner of northern peoples, and felt to be less approachable. One day Susanna sent one of her children to ask her cousin if there was any news. The child came running home as the Prussians rode noisily at full tilt into the market place, waving their pistols and with a shiny sabre between their teeth. The citizens had decided to make a friendly approach and came out of their houses, welcoming the Germans with beakers of wine. Thus peace was made and the turmoil gave way to relief. However, Susanna and Daniel were still rather uneasy because they were harbouring a young French soldier in their house. He had fallen seriously ill and was unable to start the journey home with the troops. His comrades were afraid that he would be found and, one night soon after the arrival of the Prussians, they crept through a small alley to fetch him. They called "Jules" so insistently that, sick as he was, he crawled out to them and they carried him away.

If the people thought their troubles might be lessened with what seemed to be the promise of a more stable and hopefully peaceful life, they would have another crisis to live through in the short term. This time it was not made by humans but by the very planet itself. In 1815 there was an enormous sudden eruption of the Indonesian volcano Tambora, and its ash rose to the upper spheres around the earth. With violent aftershocks for two further days, the immediate effects were spread far and wide. In the middle of summer it caused two days of darkness and, as the months went by, its influence was felt over the whole northern hemisphere. It affected the summer temperatures of 1816 so badly, with recordings in America and Europe of snow and freezing conditions in June and August, that that year's harvest was practically decimated. This was followed by another year of bad harvests, and people began to die of starvation. Whilst Susanna did her best to provide for the immediate and wider family, they had to ration their meals as best they could. On one occasion she caught her young daughter Katharina stealing some bread from the family larder. This was most unusual as Katharina was not a dishonest child but, when confronted by her mother, she sobbed that her friends were all so hungry and she could not bear it.

Susanna missed her parents greatly, her mother for her gentle grandmotherliness and her father who did much to encourage the children's education. Heinrich not only encouraged their natural curiosity and eagerness to learn; he was greatly upset by the problems in the school. Whilst the high school had a good reputation for those with academic abilities, the others were much disadvantaged. The teacher was a soldier discharged from the Dragoons who told his little flock that the life of a cowherd was preferable to that of a schoolmaster.

Some years after the death of Susanna's father, Daniel's mother was widowed and came to live with the family. She was a very strong-minded lady who had seen the introduction of the potato when she was but a child. She would tell how her teacher had brought a potato to the class, cut it up and gave it to the pupils to taste. They thought it horrible - that is, until the teacher realised that it had to be cooked. Then the children loved it and. indeed, it became a big part of the German diet. Things were not always harmonious between Susanna and her mother-in-law. The latter hung on to the old ways and was always interfering in Susanna's more progressive domestic practices and upbringing of the children.

It was a common sight in the town - Susanna taking her little brood somewhere, for all the world like a mother hen and her chicks! She put much emphasis on their musical education. The boys learnt to play different instruments - not always to the delight of the neighbours. In particular, the eldest son Jakob loved the bassoon; one neighbour offered him some money if he were to stop playing the instrument. But Jakob turned down the offer politely and continued to coax sweet tones from his bassoon. When he was older, he developed a deep bass voice.

The girls were all given singing lessons; they had good voices and often sang in harmony in the evening before bedtime. They were so good that passers-by would stop to listen, and when their talent was given glowing praise in the local newspaper, they were very proud and happy. They were to have learnt to play the piano but the teacher smoked heavily during the lessons. The smell was so strong that it made them feel ill, so they gave up their lessons. The youngest found a better teacher when she was much older and learnt to play quite well. Their repertory of songs was wide and varied, to include well-loved arias from Mozart operas and folk songs old and new.

Susanna also made sure they learnt the art of a well-run household and cooking, and they were taught to work with their hands such as sewing, embroidery and other crafts. It was not possible to buy everything, so the girls learnt to design their own embroidery and put in the colours. Their teacher was a lady from a noble family who had married a less well-heeled man for love. She was disowned by her family and her teaching helped with the budget. In winter the Steinbrecher girls learnt to spin yarn which they brought to the weaver to be turned into cloth. They would bleach this themselves and did their sewing in the summer. Gradually all three girls made their trousseau, as was the custom, and this was brought to their marriage, with just the customary damask tablecloth to be bought. All household linen was washed twice a year - in spring and autumn. Washerwomen would begin the work at 2 a.m., and the girls would help with the bleaching process and the final stages of the operation.

Spring was always uplifting and, if there was much to be done, people also took time to enjoy a walk in the countryside and the meadows full of spring flowers. On St. John's day, just after midsummer, the spring supplying the town's water was given its annual clean. This became a day the children looked forward to. When the spring had been cleared out, the children picked flowers which they put into little baskets, next to which they put eggs collected from different places. They would then take these to neighbours and friends, singing all sorts of rhymes and ditties on the way. People became happier with the sunny days, and they loved to tease and even play simple jokes on the youngsters.

As life became more stable for the region, so Susanna and Daniel were able to live more fully. They coped with their infant losses, and were much respected by the townspeople. People came to Susanna for advice when they had problems with their health and that of their children, and Daniel was actively involved in the business of the town. Susanna loved to tell how, in 1822, he was part of a deputation sent to the King of Prussia to resolve what was called the Klingenschmidt will, a scandal when several people had been arrested for fraud. The mission went to ask for the release of these people, and Daniel stood with the delegation in a dress coat, knickerbockers, silk stockings and shoes with silver buckles. Whether it was their appearance or the justification of their cause, their request was granted, and they returned home as heroes!

The last of their daughters, born in 1818, was a delicate child whom they called Carolinchen. She was much loved by them all, and they took care no harm came to her. One day Carolinchen was in school with her slightly older brother Conrad, and the teacher was about to punish her with the cane for a small misdemeanour. Conrad jumped off his chair and tore the cane out of the teacher's hand. He then broke it in two over his knee and threw the pieces down at the teacher's feet. He was so angry that he jumped out of the window and ran off. In 1831, aged just thirteen, Carolinchen was so ill that she died and was buried on Good Friday of that year. Mother Susanna was distraught and died three months later, which the family attributed to a broken heart. Daniel lived on for another ten years. His business and commercial activities were going quite well, and he was looked after at home by his daughter Sophia. The youngest child Conrad was not academic but showed an excellent talent for music. Daniel sent him to a cousin in Darmstadt who built pianos; however, first it was necessary for him to do a three-year apprenticeship in cabinet-making. At the end of this he declared he had no desire to continue as an apprentice; he went off and joined the army.

-o-o-o-o-o-o-o-o-o-o-o-o-o-

Evening had come and the two children had gone to bed. Josef sat at the table writing. His brother Carl sat by the fire, far away in thought.

"What are you writing, Josef?" he asked. "I can see the pages piling up, it must be important to you".

"Well," replied Josef. "The more I tell the children, the more comes back to me. And I remembered that our great-aunt Katharina collected all sorts of articles written in the local gazette about events that took place in Kreuznach after the Prussian rule came into force. I just thought I ought to make notes while it is fresh in my memory".

"That's a great idea", said Carl. "We are so busy living our lives when we are young. And when we want to ask the questions we should have asked then, many of the people who made up our past families are no longer there. But how come you know so much about our ancestors?"

"I suppose, being the youngest brother by quite a few years, I spent a lot more time with our parents whilst you were an apprentice. Mother knew a lot about the Steinbrechers, naturally, in fact she actually knew her grandfather Daniel. She was seven when he died, but he loved to be with his grandchildren. Then there were the times spent with Katharina. Our aunt Sophia had looked after Daniel until his death in 1841, and then she went to live with her sister Katharina. The two of them used to reminisce, and that is how the stories got told".

"That's right" agreed Carl. "I can remember hearing some of what you have told the children. Perhaps, being the eldest, I was more aware of our father's side of the family, the Holzbachers. I will give that more thought and see what I can add to the stories for Louise and Charlie. It is wonderful that they are already so interested".

Josef left his writing and went to sit opposite his brother, putting another log on to the fire for the rest of the evening.

"We have been away from Kreuznach now for a few years, and I must admit that life here in England is simpler. However, I do miss the town and our people because it was, in the main, quite a happy place for me. It is good to go back from time to time, and I hope we can do that occasionally, when our work allows".

"Yes, it is", agreed Carl. "The main thing, for me, about our life here in England is that we are not subjected to the changes in government which have never ceased to plague Rhenania. I know that our Queen Victoria has brought much of her

German heritage to bear, especially when her beloved Albert was still alive. But despite that, it is still a very different place from our homeland, and we have been made very welcome here. I heard somebody say, the other day, that half the bakers in London came originally from Germany! That is amazing! But of course, that is really why we came, isn't it? If Uncle Valentine had not come here as a young baker from Kirn, we might not have thought of it. But, when I had finished my years of training in commerce, he thought I would get further in life here in London. And eventually, when your circumstances also changed, that brought you here too".

"Well, let's hope it will be so for a long time," replied Josef. "I get the feeling that Louise is happy with her English school friends and seems to think she is as much English as they are. Charlie never says much but he has several English friends already. And they both seem to enjoy being among other children with German parents at the church activities. It is great that the German community here in Islington was able to build the Evangelical Church, so that it is possible for the children not to feel too remote from their cultural background. Did you see the picture of it in the Illustrated London News? Prince Albert made a personal nation of £300.- towards the cost of the build".

-0-0-0-0-0-0-0-0-0-0-0-

Some time later Josef went on a visit to Bad Kreuznach and Kirn, spending time with old friends and a few cousins, mainly from the Steinbrecher family. From the Reichardt family, there were none of Elise's siblings left in Kirn. Her eldest brothers had emigrated overseas, Wilhelm to Fiji and subsequently Australia and Julius to Uruguay - both having married and settled in those countries. Youngest brother Louis had also emigrated to Australia. Her younger sister Louise had come to London with her Austrian husband and since had two children.

Although his great-aunt Katharina was no longer alive, Josef spent a lot of time with her daughter Illa who was now completely blind through glaucoma. Illa was so happy to have Josef's visits, and they talked much about the family present but mostly past. Illa had lived through many events but also her brilliant memory had retained much detail of how they all lived. She was very enthusiastic about Josef's project to record all this history of the family for the young Holzbacher children and future descendants. During the long hours they spent together, Illa told Josef many more little things until he thought his brain would explode with so much to remember. Illa laughed and said she would find somebody who would be kind enough to write things down for her. She became a Roman Catholic and subsequently spent her ageing years in a convent in Belgium where she died in 1914. She did indeed find "someone kind enough", and later on

Josef received a copy of her memoirs which he found invaluable.

-0-0-0-0-0-0-0-0-0-0-0-

After he returned to London and his home with brother Carl and sister-in-law Elise, Josef continued to work on his project. With now such a wealth of information, he needed to organise it all, trying to find illustrations wherever possible. He still enjoyed his life working with Carl in the family business, and spent time with friends at the church. However, during his time in Germany, another person had come into his life and captured his heart. One autumn evening Elise found him at his writing table by the window, not writing but dreaming into the setting sun.

"Josef, I can tell you have something new on your mind. Do we need to know, or are you not ready to tell?"

"Elise, I should know that you would be sensitive to my feelings. No, I am not hiding anything from you. In fact I was just about to announce some very exciting news. Is Carl busy with anything right now?"

"No", smiled Elise. "He is just fetching his reading glasses. Ah here he comes. Carl, Josef has something exciting to tell us!"

From out of the papers on the table Josef took a photograph of an attractive young lady laughing into the camera, which was most unusual for the pictures taken by portrait photographers at the time. Mostly they looked so serious. Beaming widely Josef passed it to Elise who, also smiling, passed it on to Carl.

"Aha, my young brother. It has happened, has it? I thought you had come back to us with a twinkle in your eye, you rascal. So, come on, who is she? I see the photographer's name gives him as working in Frankfurt".

"Nothing escapes you, does it, Carl?" said Josef laughing. "Indeed she does come from Frankfurt but I met her in Bad Kreuznach - not this time but the last time I went. We have written to each other for over a year, and she came to Kreuznach again when she knew I would be there. By then we both knew we wanted to spend our lives together. She has agreed to come to England after we marry in Frankfurt next year".

"Does she have a name, by any chance?" teased Elise.

"Of course, sorry, I get so excited! Her name is Bertha, and she is smiling in the photograph because she is a happy person. She is full of joy and finds something to enjoy at every corner. She gets me doing things I would never have dreamt of doing! She says I am too quiet!!"

"Well, it sounds to me as if you are well suited", said Carl. "It will be good for you to have your own home, and I am happy to say that the business is going well enough to give you a better salary. This is indeed good news".

"Isn't it strange", said Elise, "how we are all making better lives in other countries? It is nice that so many of us have come to London. And yet our homeland is a lovely place".

"Just pushed to the limit so often by ever-changing political leaders", commented Josef. "Anyhow, in the meanwhile I shall carry on with putting the family stories together. I realised just now that the children born to us all in other countries will not know about Bad Kreuznach or Kirn, so I thought that the next part is to write as much as I know about these two places".

CHAPTER FOUR

HOW KREUZNACH FOUND FAVOUR

After the demise of Napoleon Bonaparte and the ensuing decisions of the Treaty of Vienna, Rhenania and hence the town of Kreuznach had to adjust yet again to new circumstances. Although they appreciated the peace that seemed to have come, the people knew it was still fragile. How many decades, not to say centuries, had their ancestors had to endure the effects of ambitious kings and emperors disputing the territories of Rhenania? They could not imagine that this was suddenly to be a thing of the past, but their natural optimism and resourcefulness allowed them to push troubled waters to one side and rebuild their lives and livelihoods.

For Kreuznach it was to be the saltworks which would give a huge boost to the town. Although the story subsequently passed into oblivion, originally it was a shepherd by the name of Wilhelmy who, in his simple way, drew attention to the waters. He kept his sheep up in the hills, at the very top where nature had gone wild but where there was a spring. From its stream a branch had made it possible to dig a mill pond. When he heard people wondering about saline water, Wilhelmy maintained that there was a saline spring on the banks of the stream. He said that the stones were covered in rust and that there was a not very pleasant smell, but that his sheep always went to certain spots there to lick the salt water. Everyone knew that sheep love salt but, nevertheless, they thought Wilhelmy was not exactly an idiot but a simpleton - what would he know? Despite being laughed at and held up as a joke, Wilhelmy followed his instinct until he found a saline spring that actually flowed into the river Nahe itself.

This was the beginning of the town as a spa resort. The saline spring in the river was harnessed, the spa gardens were laid out, a wooden bathing house was built, and a few stalls set out. As time went by, an avenue of poplar trees was cut down, which gave place to pathways for people and a road for vehicles. A small house was built for the shepherd Wilhelmy and his daughters were the first so-called "spa ladies". Quick to take advantage, some people offered board and lodging to visitors to the spa, the hotel accommodation was improved, and all this attracted aristocrats and other wealthy people come to bathe in the therapeutic waters. In time new bathing facilities were built and, in 1834, a company was established to run the increasing activity of the resort. The radon properties of the water were discovered and it was medically endorsed as beneficial for rheumatic disorders.

But as the decades went by, the geographically strategic position of the town, now called Bad Kreuznach, would continue to bring unrest and strife, and people felt that they could never truly live in peace. The railway came to Bad Kreuznach in the middle of the 19th century purported to be for touristic purposes. However, even a century after it was built, its strategic importance was primarily its reason for being.

-0-0-0-0-0-0-0-0-0-0-0-

THE CHRONICLE OF KATHARINA (STEINBRECHER) MAURER 1805-1883

The first child of Susanna and Daniel Steinbrecher to survive infancy was eldest daughter Katharina. She was a very healthy child, full of energy and highly intelligent. As a child she was extremely lively and always outdoors on adventures. She climbed like a squirrel which sometimes could have been disastrous. On one occasion, when helping with the haymaking on a relative's farm, she climbed into the hayloft and fell through a hole into the freshly stacked piles of hay. She fell so deeply that she was almost smothered by the hay.

Katharina loved to explore the world around her and seized every opportunity to go further afield. On one excursion to a place called Oppenheim, she climbed high up into the church tower - so high that she got lost. The sexton was none too thrilled when he had to climb up to bring her down again. During this same excursion she visited the Oppenheim ossuary, made up of the bones of Swedish soldiers killed during a war more than a century previously. It made a lasting impression on her.

Responsive to the teaching of her grandfather Heinrich, and to all that her mother Susanna brought to her children's upbringing, Katharina gathered knowledge as a sponge soaks up water. Whilst as a child, she loved to tease her brothers and sisters with gentle humour, in later life she became the centre of the family, welcoming all those in need of love and kindness. When she was a young teenager, grandfather Heinrich arranged for her to go with some of his relatives through many new places and ultimately to Frankfurt. Walking for most of the way, they reached Mainz where the river Main flows into the mighty Rhine. From Mainz they were able to get passage on a market boat going up the Main to Frankfurt. The boat was pulled by horses along the bank of the river, so there was plenty of time to look at the new countryside. From time to time the vessel would get stuck on a sand bank, and they would have to wait until waves were sufficiently high to re-float the boat. They were joined along the route by a group of musicians, and so there was a lot of fun for all on the slow journey to the city of Frankfurt. Katharina had been given a letter of recommendation by her father for a landlord he was acquainted with in the city. However, her relatives were reluctant to stay in town and insisted on walking to nearby Friedberg where they found modest overnight lodgings. The next day was Whitsunday, and Katharina never forgot the wonderful spring day and meadows of beautiful spring flowers she saw everywhere.

Katharina got married in 1833 to Joseph Maurer. The eldest son of a farmer, the young Joseph wanted to become a solicitor and got a place at a grammar school where he was able to finish his education. However, he then had to serve with the Prussian army liberating the region from Napoleon. He rose to the rank of sergeant-major and was awarded a medal. After this he was discharged as a lieutenant in the territorial army, where he served for some years and left with the rank of captain. Upon returning to Kreuznach he became a solicitor's managing clerk, and it was while attending an auction on behalf of his employer that he first met Katharina.

Joseph was shy and unsure of himself. Although they had subsequently met again at a dance, he afterwards found an opportunity to visit the Steinbrecher household. Katharina had also fallen for Joseph but, as he was not forthcoming, she presumed he must be interested in someone else. However, one day he went again to the Steinbrecher house. In an awkward conversation Joseph told Katharina he was thinking of getting married. Katharina was in turmoil but she managed to tell him that was quite a natural thing for him to want. He then told her she knew his intended bride and wanted to show her who it was. He led her to a mirror and, of course, she saw straightaway who he meant - upon which he asked the big question, and they became engaged.

Joseph and Katharina married and settled in the town. Joseph was an honest and kind man who always gave help to orphans and widows if he could. He could not abide bad-mouthing or lies and, if he had to hurt people through business, he would find a way to soften the blow. One instance of this was when a fisherman took some gravel from a part of the river bank belonging to a builder. This was against the law firstly because the land belonged to someone else, but also because it caused damage to the river bank which was always at risk during floods. The fisherman was arrested and punished according to the law but, later on, Joseph gave him a suit of clothes.

The first child born to Katharina and Joseph in 1834 was a girl they named Elisabeth, whom they always called Illa. There was also a baby son some three years later but he died at only 6 weeks. No more children were to complement the Maurer household, but philosophical Katharina devoted her maternal instincts not just to her beloved Illa but also to orphaned children who needed a temporary home. She delighted in making their Christmas celebrations special for the little ones, and would set out toy animals and even put a glass dish full of water and moss as a pond for the toy ducks and swans. When her father died in 1841, her sister Sophia came to live with her, having looked after him and remaining unmarried. She had fallen in love once, been unable to marry her chosen soulmate and had not wanted to choose anyone else. Katharina was glad of her presence within the family. They shared the household skills instilled in them by Susanna, their mother. However, Sophia reigned supreme in the kitchen, and she gave training to a good many of the local young girls in the art of cookery. For the family she was a blessing as she also possessed wonderful nursing skills which unfortunately were called upon quite often.

Meanwhile Joseph was carving out an excellent career. He soon became recognised as a very good legal adviser and very quickly was spotted by the Puricelli family who offered him a 20-year contract to become their business manager. The Puricellis were a very important employer in Rheinböllen, a town just a few miles from Kreuznach. The first Puricelli migrated from lake Como in Italy to Kreuznach in the early 1750s. His son married the daughter of an industrialist called Utsch in Rheinböllen. She inherited the Utsch iron ore works employing many local people, and subsequent sons were to run not just those works but also gas works developed around the area. The Puricelli family had a great social conscience, comparable to the Cadbury family in England, except that they were not Quakers but staunch Roman Catholics. They set up an orphanage, a hospital, and a service for mentally ill adults over the age of 40 - the latter most unusual for the era when the mentally ill were mostly locked up in mental institutions. The trust buildings comprised the management offices, a gatehouse which served also as a munitions store, a so-called "casino" which was a kind of leisure centre, the gardener's quarters and a family chapel. Its existence can be traced down the years and received protection under the Hague Convention.

In Kreuznach the spa company was gaining in momentum, and the town saw quite a few of the rich and famous come to take the waters. Karl Marx had his wedding there in 1843, and Clara Schumann and her sister gave a concert there on one occasion. There was also a cross-section of princesses, duchesses and countesses, with or without their husbands. Some of Josef's Maurer relatives took on the hotel "Zum Pariser Hof" built in 1840, and there were quite a few tales to be heard about the eccentricities of the aristocracy. One day Katharina and Josef had decided to take their small daughter on a steamer going from Kastel some way down the Rhine. They got on the boat but it did not occur to them until they were well underway that there were few other passengers. Josef went to ask the ship's captain about the reason for this only to hear that they had climbed aboard a special boat belonging to the Prussian prince who later became Kaiser Wilhelm I. Illa later told how she had a vague recollection of a stately gentleman sitting on deck and beckoning to her. However, she would not go to him because she preferred playing games with some of his entourage!

In 1844 the town was hit once again by flooding. Despite the news being spread rapidly that the river Nahe was rising fast, some children were unable to get home from school and had to spend the night in the classroom. The doctor tried to get to some people but his carriage was too light to cope with the rushing water. Another driver came with his heavy omnibus drawn by horses, but the vehicle was too heavy for them. They were quickly taken out of their harnesses and brought to safety, whilst the carriage had to be left to its fate in the water. People were running around doing what they could to save others. Katharina's brother Conrad worked long and hard in the powerful floodwater, and he managed to save the lives of three people. He later suffered badly from rheumatism, and this was attributed largely to the time he had spent in the river. The next morning the waters had subsided, but there was a great deal of damage. Plaster had been ripped from the walls of houses - of which three had been completely washed away. Many belongings were to be seen washed up into trees.

In 1848 another revolution broke out in Paris, and king Louis-Philippe was dethroned. A republic was declared, and unrest spread once more eastwards from France towards the Rhine river. The population again feared that Rhenania would be invaded by the French, and in its towns and cities guards were formed called local defence volunteers. These were made up of ordinary citizens, all of whom were anxious to defend their freedom and territory. Josef Maurer announced that, were there to be war against the French, he would enlist to fight for his homeland. Indeed, in Bad Kreuznach a unit was set up and Josef was elected as its captain and commandant.

Exercises were carried out, and even the most unlikely men had to learn how to wield a flintlock gun and other weapons. The younger teenage boys in the town became overexcited; they divided into two sides, one on each side of the river, and got into such fights that the police had to be called to sort them out.

Not to be outdone, the women of Kreuznach embroidered a wonderful flag with the town's coat of arms in blue and silver. The inaugural ceremony took place on the so-called Whitsun meadow, and afterwards - under escort from the town band - the flag was brought to the commandant's house to be available when needed. Then the mayor of the town took it away and proclaimed it could only be used for public events. His decision was soon to be overturned because, some time later, black-red-gold (the regional colours on the flag) was prohibited and replaced with black-white-red. Political parties got involved, and the liberals (who had been irritated when the flag had been removed from the commandant) put in a complaint for its return. The judge declared himself incompetent on account of the value of the flag and, with this comfortable excuse, brought the proceedings to an end. The disputed trophy passed into obscurity, and was wrapped up in a corner of the town hall.

The fear of invasion and unrest continued in the region. Some became patriotic to the extreme; some citizens in the defence units became militarist and wanted march-pasts and the like. As in Heinrich Paul's time, vandalism and protection rackets started up. Some businessmen paid up for a while, then became impatient and refused. Gangs then smashed windows and ranted through the town intent on plunder. As commandant still, Josef Maurer was called upon to deal with the hooligans, and his personality was such that he commanded respect even from the wrongdoers. On one occasion a crowd of people had come from elsewhere and gathered outside the city walls. Their intention was to enter the town, depose the officials and demand work and food. Josef decided it was better to go and meet them rather than allow them entry. Other officials had already tried to turn them away but were shouted down as soon as they tried to speak. Josef chose another way; he stood in front of them until they were ready to listen. He told them that, as they were well aware, there was no work or extra food but, if they showed themselves to be amenable and pleasant, an effort would be made to find work for them. And then they would be able to buy food wherever available. The crowd had respect for Josef and agreed to do as he suggested for the time being. However, the unrest festered on; agitators vandalised the crosses on the town's bridge. When they were arrested, another angry crowd threatened to storm the prison and set them free. Josef once again managed to calm them down.

A new constitution was brought in and representatives of the Democratic Party went to Josef, as commandant, to demand that the civil defence guards swear allegiance to the new rule. Josef was not convinced that the new constitution would last long and refused the request. He maintained that it would only bring more unhappiness to Kreuznach because it would be under occupation once more. Under this new rule general decisions were taken by the Frankfurt parliament. However, after a high profile shooting, its members had fled to Stuttgart and carried on there as a temporary government called the "Rumpf Parliament". Nevertheless the partisans occupied certain positions in the Rhineland area, and the Prussian army was stationed down river from Kreuznach. Their looks of hatred crossed the waters to the town but fortunately, at that point, they did not invade. Threats continued to arrive against the defence unit and on Josef's own house. The Puricelli family and their community was also threatened with attack and, for two weeks, Josef had to maintain order and prepare in case of aggression. Happily things went without incident and gradually peace, fragile though it was, returned.

But the earth itself decided to revolt as well and, some time later, a huge tremor shook the town one evening. Doors rattled, crockery fell off shelves, houses began to sway and the church bells rang themselves. People fled from their houses. However, the quake ceased, the damage was minimal, and the townspeople returned gratefully to their homes.

In 1851 Katharina had to bear the loss of her beloved Josef who succumbed to ill health and fatigue. Worse was to come when her only child Illa went blind after contracting glaucoma. Katharina took her to see a famous professor by the name of Graefe in Berlin, but he could do nothing for the young girl. Illa was naturally distraught but finally found peace of mind and confort in her religion. Meanwhile, thanks to the success of the family hotel, Katharina was able to employ an professional governess for her daughter. This lady was very sensitive to Illa's condition. She not only read to her but also enabled Illa to continue with her music - she had learnt to play the piano beautifully already from childhood. The governess would read out the notes to Illa, who would then practise and learn them by heart. As time went by she was able to play some of the most difficult pieces by Beethoven and other composers. So, in 1865, Katharina gave her a Bechstein piano. It was mainly in this way that Illa reached her spiritual equilibrium. But she also had a wonderful sense of humour and loved to hear new stories. She had a fantastic memory and retained many of these and other children's tales, which she then took delight in relating to the little ones. Katharina and her sister Sophia died in the 1880s, and it was some years later that Illa decided to live her life in a Belgian convent until she died in 1914.

-0-0-0-0-0-0-0-0-0-0-0-

Carl and Josef were chatting one day. Things were going reasonably well with the business which Carl had taken over from his previous employer Charles Westphal. Quite a few people had found some prosperity during the reign of Queen Victoria who was about to celebrate sixty years on the throne. The family relationship between the British royal family and German royalty was cordial. Since the 1850s Queen Victoria and her prime ministers had evolved a policy of "splendid isolation" which aimed at not interfering in the affairs of any of the European nations who were still constantly warring with each other.

Britain had become very powerful with its enormous empire, and the development of many big industries had brought fortune to owners and investors. Some of the wealthy employers thought about the condition of the people they relied on to do this often hard and dirty work and, if ensuring their wellbeing was not altogether altruistic, it nevertheless improved the lives of many. Children of all backgrounds now had the right to a minimal education until they were 12 or even 14 later on. This prosperity of sorts led to higher expectancy over the years and, among the more affluent, there had grown a demand for previously unattainable luxuries such as toilet soap and perfumes, to name but two. This in turn was advantageous to manifold allied businesses, of which Carl's was one. Essential oils were highly important in the manufacture of those particular luxury goods, besides other more obscure uses.

"To return to my project, the final Steinbrecher I want to write about is our maternal grandfather, Carl", said Josef.

"But neither you or I ever knew him - or for that matter any of our grandparents", said Carl.

"Yes, that is right and that is why I thought it important to record the little we know of those directly responsible for our being here!"

CHAPTER FIVE

THE CHRONICLE OF JACOB STEINBRECHER
(1807 - 1855)

Jacob was younger than Katharina by two years and the first son of the surviving Steinbrecher children. He was a very lovable and highly intelligent little boy. However, as he grew older he became increasing wilful and this caused much concern to his parents. But he was an excellent pupil at the local high school and was thought to have a future career of promise. As already related, his father Daniel ran a busy china shop and glazing business, and Jacob was called upon to help from time to time. It was quite normal at the time for older children to do so, and so one day Jacob was required by his father to help set up a stall at the annual fair. A note had been written excusing his absence from school, but it was mislaid and, when he went to his class the next day, he was given a punishment of extra dictation. Jacob was very upset not because of the dictation but because he had not been believed when he tried to explain. After this he refused to set foot inside the high school ever again, and no threat or entreaty from his parents could make him change his mind. Even though the headmaster made a visit to the family and made much of Jacob's talents, he had no more success than the parents. Jacob said he would rather jump off the bridge into the cold waters of the river Nahe.

He remained at home and became a glazier under his father's tuition. Then, as all young men were, he was called up to do military service in the Prussian army. It was as a recruit in Mainz that he met his future wife Marie whom he subsequently made very happy. After his military duties came to an end, the couple returned to Bad Kreuznach. They had two children, a son Jean who was a telegraph operator in civilian life and, when conscripted in 1870 in yet another Franco-Prussian war, made a career as such in the Prussian army. Jacob and Marie also had a daughter Regine. Jacob became an innkeeper and his inn, recognisable by its archway, stood opposite the evangelical church orphanage. As already related in the chronicle of Susanna and her children, Jacob had a love of the bassoon and had developed a wonderful but rough bass voice. He loved singing to entertain his customers.

Jacob was at last settled and happy in his life but he nevertheless still retained the unruly streak which had brought him so many problems previously. He might well have lived for many more years if, at the age of 48 in 1855, he had not made a foolish bet. He maintained that he could lift a heavy barrel on his own - whereby he twisted his gut and died a very painful death. If the wider Steinbrecher family was much saddened by this unnecessary turn of events, Jacob's wife was devastated. She carried on running the inn but, one year later, it was announced that the concession would not be given to a woman with a widow's status. On the steps of the town hall, where she had just been given this awful news, this further shock was such that she was struck down by a massive stroke and died on the spot. The inn was subsequently demolished.

No more is known of Jean Steinbrecher, except that he married but had no children. His sister Regine had some trauma from her childhood when she was attacked in the garden by a very aggressive cock. The bird was trying to peck out her eyes, and her screams brought her father running to protect her. In true Jacob style, he caught the angry bird and immediately wrung its neck. Regine was seriously ill from the shock and, very strangely, one of her legs stopped growing. This left her with a permanent limp. In 1856, at the age of 22, she married a post office clerk from Kirn, Carl Christian Holzbacher, and this is the family tie leading to Carl and Josef Holzbacher now living in London.

-0-0-0-0-0-0-0-0-0-0-0-

"Sad, isn't it? To think that, but for that stupid prank, we might have known him" said Carl.

"Yes, even you were born two years only after he died. Did mother ever mention him?"

"Not really" replied Carl. "But they all loved him. He might have been a bit of a rebel, more of a problem to himself really, although it did affect others. Katharina said that he was always such fun and a very affectionate brother and uncle to her little Illa. His daughter Regine - our mother - was born only a short while after Illa and they knew each other very well. She was a quieter child than Illa who was always so lively".

Josef had been in the middle of writing more of his project. "You know, Carl", he said after a while. "There are so many anecdotes about all our ancestors that it is difficult to keep a focus of who is who and where! And they all had the same first names, or nearly, a bit like you and me - and our brother Valentine. But before we tell the children more about their grandparents, as far as we can, and since your Elise also comes from Kirn, I think I must set out what kind of little town Kirn was".

CHAPTER SIX

KIRN, THE TOWN KNOWN AS THE PLACE OF "LEATHER, STONE AND BEER"

Over the centuries the town of Kirn had mixed fortunes, and was less affluent in good times than Kreuznach. The name derives possibly from the celtic "kyr" meaning water; another possible origin is the germanic word Keere meaning mill. Both are logical since the town has two rivers, the Nahe and the Hahnenbach which provided either transport for goods (and people), water for animals, and an abundance of fish. They enabled watermills to work, for milling grain and cereals produced in the region. One strong product came from the quarries near the town, where the quartz was particularly good (melaphyre). This gave employment to miners and the product to agate polishers in the times when agate was prized in the jewellery trade, in decorative crafts such as the burnishing of applied gold leaf, and other fields. The quartz also filtered the water which was especially pure, and this in turn gave rise to the tanning of leather and the brewing of good beer. There were three tanneries which were very productive for quite a few decades and, in the mid-1800s, employed over 1,000 workers. The beer had a good reputation and one of its brewers, Bernhard Stroh, went out to America in the mid-1800s and founded what was, for a while, the third largest brewery of the USA, established in Detroit. In passing, it should perhaps be mentioned that he was not the only German brewer to do so. After the uprising of 1848, a number of disillusioned Prussian brewers went to Illinois and set up breweries, particularly in Milwaukee.

Kirn acquired town status with the relevant civil rights in 1857. It had a Jewish population already in the middle ages which, for some reason, disappeared in the 15th century but gradually returned in the 18th century. In 1866 the Jewish community was formally established, and some of the men were "empowered to exercise the franchise". There followed the building of a synagogue, a Jewish school and "mikveh" or Jewish graveyard. A final quirky piece of information: the infamous Schinderhannes (mentioned extensively in Chapter 2), whose real name was Johann Bückler, was born in Kirn and, as a teenager, was jailed for thieving in Kirn prison - but he escaped during his first night there!

-0-0-0-0-0-0-0-0-0-0-0-

Carl and Josef were in the garden, picking vegetables and harvesting some of the soft fruit just come into season. The family were expecting visitors, including the much loved Uncle Valentine Holzbacher and his English wife Ann. Young Charlie was feeding the chickens and looking for freshly laid eggs. His older sister Louise was with her mother Elise in the kitchen, helping to prepare the food for the big family lunch they were all looking forward to. Elise's sister Louise, usually called Louie, and her husband Stephen Goermer had joined the family some time ago and were living on the top floor of the house. Stephen was a very able Austrian waiter whom Louie had met when she went to work in Switzerland and train in the hotel industry. They were now both qualified and had also come to England, where they thought things would give them more scope in the hospitality trade. Also coming to join the family were two uncles of Elise and Louie, John and Philipp Turck, who had been in London for quite a few years, and their families. John was a baker who had gone out to Australia in about 1860, married and had two children there, then brought his family to London where they ran a bakery. Philipp joined him, but not in the bakery. He was an accountant in a London bank.

The meal had been planned especially for Josef who was about to go to Frankfurt to marry his beloved Bertha. It was to be a simple wedding with just Bertha's relatives, and then the couple would come to live in London - at first with Carl and Elise until Josef had found a place for them. He wanted Bertha to be with him to choose their first home together.

With the preparations almost finished, and the dining table extended to cater for the large party, a loud knocking heralded the last of the guests to arrive - Uncle Valentine and Aunt Ann. Their arms were full of goodies. Uncle Valentine was beloved by all the family for his larger-than-life personality, and they had the greatest respect for how he and his wife had worked long and hard to achieve their present comfortable status. The couple's greatest sorrow was not to have been blessed with children, and they made much of Carl's growing family. Valentine was generous to a fault with both adults and children, and the latter always remembered him (and especially what they perceived as his large nose!) with much affection long after he was no longer around.

"Where is little Elsa?" he asked. "And my lovely Louise - how grown up you are these days. And here's our young man of the house - why, I declare you have grown bigger than I was at your age, Charlie my boy".

Aunt Ann headed straight to the kitchen with a huge bag full of bread and rolls. "Baked this morning" she said proudly as she gave them to Elise.

"Thank you" said Elise. "But you are supposed to be retired now and let others do your baking!"

"Well, yes, I know. And the shops we sold on are doing very well, I am glad to say. But I still have to learn how to be a lady of leisure. And I see you have some helpers?"

"Yes, this is my sister Louie who has come over from Switzerland with her husband Stephen - though his name is actually Etienne. They are in the hotel trade and came here last month. They are staying with us while they find their feet".

"Hello Louie, it is good to see that Elise has some of her own family here now. We Holzbachers have been so many, she must have longed to see you".

The two sisters nodded, beaming widely, and Elise added "and what is more, our brother Christian intends to come as well".

After all the greetings were over, the family settled in the dining room to enjoy their meal. The talk went to Josef's wedding in Germany, and he explained that it was to be a quiet event with just Bertha's family and some friends. He said that he was looking forward to bringing his bride back with him. There would be another family occasion where everyone would have a chance to get to know her. When asked whether he would be visiting relatives in Kreuznach, he replied that he would stop briefly on his way to Frankfurt, mainly to see Illa before she went to the convent in Belgium.

At this point Uncle Valentine told them all of his journey, with his wife and some friends, when they had spent weeks travelling by boat and train to visit all up and down the Rhine. They had even ventured down into Switzerland where they had enjoyed lakes and mountains. None of the others present had ever gone so far except for Louie who had lived some time in German-speaking Switzerland, working in hotels. They were all eager to hear about other places, and Elise said that she had started to collect the postcards sent by family and friends from their travels. In particular she loved the artistic ones, drawn and coloured by hand, which seemed so much more romantic than the photographed ones.

"I'm going to ask Illa to do something for me", announced Josef. "As some of you already know, I have been putting together many of the stories handed down to us by our ancestors. Some while ago our lovely young Louise asked where we came from, and that gave me the impetus to write it down while there are many people to fill in the details. As you all know, Illa and her mother Katharina were great ones for talking about the family. I know Illa can no longer write herself because of her blindness, but perhaps she could find someone at the convent to assist her in recording all she knows. I am sure she would love to think she can give this to our children and to all those who will follow".

Young Louise was listening avidly to the conversations. She loved it when the family came together, especially as it was rare to have so many of them at one time. And this encouraged her to ask Uncle Valentine if he could also write down the story of how he grew up in Germany.

Thus it came about that Valentine wrote his own story, and so here is the next chronicle.

CHAPTER SEVEN

THE CHRONICLE OF GEORG VALENTIN
HOLZBACHER (1833 - 1919) Part one

Although named Georg for his grandfather, he was always called Valentin. Born in 1833 in Kirn, he was the last of six children, third son and younger than the first child by sixteen years. His ancestors had come to Kirn in the 17th century and were the town millers for three generations. His grandparents had been bakers in the town and had made a comfortable living, providing some financial wealth and enabling the purchase of some land and property. However they had died within six months of each other when Valentine's father Georg Jacob was only ten years old.

As the only son Georg Jacob stood to receive a good inheritance. Whilst he was still under age, this was entrusted to his mother's brothers Jacob and Philip Ackva, also millers in the town of Kirn. They kept back some of the inheritance but sent Georg Jacob to college to be trained as a chemist. He also learnt Latin, spoke not only his native German but also French fluently, and was later very good in his profession. However as a student he led a frivolous life, spending his money too freely on drinking and making merry. He got married aged thirty to Marie Elisabeth Ackva, only daughter of the town miller and only fifteen years of age.

Valentine's parents settled in Kirn where all six children were born. By the time Valentine came into the world, his father - ever the spendthrift - had sold one piece of land after another until all that was left was the freehold cottage in which they lived. Although Georg Jacob was good at his work, conscientious and honest, he was too fond of drinking, although he never did so whilst at work. The children had respect for his intelligence and honesty and, even when drunk, he never laid a finger on any of his family. His eldest sister Sophie helped her mother look after the family, as did the other sister Christina. The second child, also a sister, had died in infancy. Valentine's brothers Jacob and Christian Carl were respectively six and three years older than him, so he was often left to his own devices. His earliest recollection was around the age of two; standing with his mother outside their house, a policeman came up to her and said "You must send your boy to school tomorrow morning". Valentine was very frightened but his mother explained that the policeman meant his brother Christian Carl who was five and obliged to attend school from then on.

Being the youngest child, and a boy to boot, Valentine always wanted to do the same as the other boys. He never saw danger in anything and became quite accident-prone as a consequence, The first happened when, as a four year old, he was standing on the river bank. Cows were grazing in the same field and some came down to the river's edge to drink. For some reason one of them decided to toss Valentine into the air, and he landed on his head. Luckily a woman was nearby and ran to pick him up. With blood streaming down his face and clothes, she carried him home to be cared for. Another time, when accompanying his brother Christian Carl who was carrying a basket of goods to his mother, Valentine ran too close to the wall and stumbled on a stone sticking out. He cut his chin so badly that he could put his finger in the wound, and had the scar to show for the rest of his life.

Further accidents happened when he was out with his young friends. Playing in the nearby forest once, he fell out of a tree on to his head and shoulder. If the ground had not been wet and soft, he would doubtless have fractured his skull. Two of the boys took off their jackets to put under his head, whilst another ran home to fetch brother Jacob and a neighbour. They came with a large sheet on which to carry him home. The doctor was called and examined him; luckily there were no broken bones but his spine was badly hurt, and this was confirmed by another doctor called when he was no better a few days later. They both told Valentine he had been very lucky; as he had lain on the wet ground for over an hour and then carried for about two miles in the sheet, they said he was very fortunate to still be alive and should be more careful in future. As it was, Valentine was in bed for about two weeks and then went happily back to his childhood life!

The two rivers of the town provided good sport for the boys both in summer and winter. They went fishing in both rivers, and caught plentiful supplies to take home; one of the biggest any of them ever caught weighed about 3 lbs. Disaster nearly struck Valentine again when he was about nine years old. He had gone swimming with his cousin and some other boys, and his cousin pushed him into the deepest water and left him. When he rose to the surface for the second time, another boy saw him and pulled him out. So he did not drown but learnt a valuable lesson - if you do not panic under water, it will lift you up without any effort on your part.

In the winter the rivers froze over sufficiently for the boys to go skating. When Valentine was ten years old, the winter was so severe that the rivers were frozen for almost five months and the ice was nearly two feet thick. But when the ice started to break up and the snow on the hills began to melt, the rivers swelled to overflowing. The Nahe, which runs through the town, totally overflowed its banks and the whole of Kirn was flooded. For some hours the Holzbacher family home was under water to about two feet high. They watched the river from their upstairs window; there were large blocks of ice floating and colliding in the river, and the sound was horrendous. Every now and then a house was swept away into the waters, and everyone was terrified. The people were dealing with the aftermath and damage for months to come.

In 1842 Valentine's mother died. He never forgot her passing and how the whole family was by her bedside at the end. Suddenly father Georg Jacob said "she is dead" and the children all burst into tears. But through the commotion their mother roused and said very clearly "I am not dead yet". Indeed she did not die until the following morning, and Georg Jacob then explained that she had been ice cold and stiff when he had spoken, and he could not imagine that she would be able to speak. The eldest daughter Sophie was used to looking after the household and took over, with her younger sister Christina, the running of family affairs. Georg Jacob was now working in Kreuznach as assistant chemist and did not always return home after long days at the pharmacy. Jacob was in Kirn, working in the extensive leather industry, essentially making shoes. Carl Christian turned fourteen in 1844 and began his training as a clerk with the post office in Bad Kreuznach. So, all in all, the family continued without too many practical worries - that is until 1845, when Sophie died of tuberculosis, a disease which took many lives at the time. This left Christina, Jacob and Valentine living in Kirn, with father Georg Jacob and Carl Christian coming home when they could.

Valentine was at school in Kirn from the age of five to the usual leaving age of fourteen. He was a regular if unexceptional student; indeed the only acceptable excuse for absence was illness or death in the family. However, on one occasion after school was finished for the day, Valentine walked to Kreuznach to see his father. This was some eight miles and took about two hours. He stayed overnight and left at five o'clock the next morning to be back in Kirn in time for school. He thought he would take a shortcut but lost his way completely; instead of two hours, it took him four. He did not go home but went straight to his class - where the schoolmaster made him stand in the corner for an hour! Valentine did not think this was unjustified, nor that the teacher had any ill feeling towards him. There were about 100 boys at the school and Valentine held his own if he did not shine particularly. However, he must have been appreciated at least for good behaviour as he recalls being the only one to receive a hymn book as a leaving prize.

Carl Christian was doing well in the Kreuznach post office where he was considered to be a good trainee - he certainly wrote a good hand. The postmaster also ran the main hotel in the town and, on occasion, a guest arrived at the hotel and needed someone to show them the way to another neighbouring village. If it was on a Sunday, Carl would fetch his young brother to act as guide and carry the bags. So it was, one Sunday morning, Valentine accompanied a lady and carried her carpet bag to Herstein, a village some eight miles from the town and partly uphill. When they were approaching their destination, the lady said she did not require him any longer. She opened her purse and gave him three pfennigs but Valentine saw she had plenty of silver. He told her it was not enough because he would have to walk sixteen miles that day, carrying a heavy bag for eight of them, and that with no dinner. So she added three more pfennigs! Another time Jacob was with Valentine because a clergyman needed them to carry a heavy box to a neighbouring village. The lads had to go through the forest for some of the way; it was late afternoon and getting dark, and every so often they would stumble and fall. Jacob took the lead and encouraged his young brother, saying they would get out of the forest in a short while. They did indeed soon arrive at their destination. The clergyman was very pleased and gave each of them six pfennigs; he also lent them a lantern for the return journey. In the summer of 1846 there was an extraordinarily good fruit harvest, especially of apples. Everyone who could made large barrels of cider, and it was the best that anyone had ever tasted. The apples were so plentiful that they were selling in large baskets for three pfennigs at the local market.

    Valentine's childhood had been no more difficult than many of those around him. It came to an end in 1847 when he turned fourteen. After the compulsory confirmation, obligatory in any Christian denomination, he was sent to live with an uncle who had a flour mill. It was very hard work, with long hours. He had to work both at the mill and in the fields. His first winter at the mill was very severe, and Valentine's uncle was surprised and pleased at his nephew's resistance to the inclement weather. They grew quite attached to one another, and Valentine did not mind that his uncle was very strict. At the end of the first year, the uncle placed Valentine as apprentice to a baker in Kirn called Simon, who was one of the mill's best customers.

His apprenticeship was to last three years and had to bee paid for. Simon was not a pleasant person, and Valentine thought he would have made a good slave driver. The apprentices had much to suffer from this irritable, bad-tempered man, who was also mean, selfish and insensitive. Work started in the bakehouse at about 2 a.m. and continued relentlessly until dinnertime. After this the apprentices were sent to the fields to work until so-called sponge time at about 7 p.m. This was the routine on every day except Sundays - when they had to bake double the amount of rolls and cakes, so that work was never finished before dinnertime. Valentine worked alongside an older apprentice. When they were sent to the fields the people working there, also employees of the baker Simon, felt sorry for the boys. They thought the boys should not have to work day and night, and suggested they should lie down in a corner of the field for some sleep. They kept watch but, on the only two occasions the apprentices did so, the master found out and created merry hell for them all, so they never did it again.

Usually the apprentices slept on the bakehouse floor, their beds consisting of sacks filled with husks and without blankets. They were woken in the very early morning by the night-watchman tapping on the bakehouse window. If they did not get up immediately, the master would come in and rouse the older apprentice with a kicking - it was only his uncle's intervention which prevented Valentine from getting the same treatment. The master's wife tried to help and told her husband that it was very cruel to make apprentices work day and night. She was told to mind her own business, that it had nothing to do with her. One day the older apprentice could no longer bear things; that day he had received three beatings - one from the master, one from the master's brother and another from the master's father. Before he left, he told Valentine "Mark my words - when I have gone, Simon will have to get up in the night to hep you make the dough. And if he does, he will be a dead man within two weeks".

And indeed, it happened exactly as the apprentice had predicted. Two weeks later, the baker died of rapid consumption. Valentine could feel no sadness at his master's death, and it did not take long before things took a turn for the better. The mistress was a very different person and had the kindest of hearts. She would not let him sleep on the bakehouse floor any longer, but gave him a nice bed upstairs. She told him that he did not have to work in the fields any more, unless he wanted to. He did occasionally do this and, whenever he did, the baker's wife would have a meal ready for him. If he got home too late for that, she would give him a small bottle of the local wine instead. Mrs. Simon employed a manager for six months and, when he left, she gave his job to Valentine who was not yet sixteen years old. When Valentine's uncle heard about it, he thought it wonderful that his nephew had done so well so quickly.

Valentine stayed as manager for another two years, and his wages brought in 2 schillings a week, plus board and lodging, which was reckoned to be quite good. Under his management they baked double the quantity of rolls, not because they were better than previously but because they were bigger. Simon had always made them smaller than the other bakeries because he was so mean - as Valentine said, he was pennywise and pound-foolish. But Valentine believed, for some time already, that he could do better for himself. He had thought about going to England quite a while previously, when he heard that many others like him had done so. Simon had always spoken disparagingly about it - probably because he thought to influence his own apprentices. He told them that he had been there himself (which he never substantiated) that the work was too hard and the hours too long. He said that he used to sweat so much that his shoes were full of water. Valentine did not doubt that this might well be true, but he reckoned that things were not better at the Kirn bakery.

So he continued to reflect on what he might do. Military service was compulsory, but he could volunteer for the army and enlist for nine or twelve years. He thought that, once his service had come to an end, he would be eligible for a position in government service for life, which was a rule in the German army. This prospect induced a good many young men not to wait for conscription but to enlist voluntarily. One day, as he walked through the town, he made up his mind and was about to begin the appropriate steps, when he was stopped by a business acquaintance who suggested a chat. He asked Valentine a lot of questions, including how much he was currently earning. After further discussion, and learning how much Valentine was being paid, he suggested to him that he should go to England. He reminded Valentine of young bakers of the same age that he had known locally and told him they were earning nearly four times as much. This settled the issue of his future for Valentine and, the next time he saw his father, he told him he would be emigrating to England - and found no objection to his decision. Despite the relative economic improvement in Rhenania, there had been another uprising in 1848, and the centuries-old quarrel between the French and the Prussians for possession of the area had never gone away. Nobody felt safe from further military conflict and the inevitable changes in administration which came with occupation, from whatever side.

-0-0-0-0-0-0-0-0-0-0-0-

From the beginning of the 19th century many people began to emigrate mostly to the new world - America and Australia to name but two. They went from all over Europe, seeking what promised to be a better chance in life. The same was true of Rhenania as more and more young men, in particular, found themselves perhaps with work but without hope of improvement; they also had had enough of the years taken from them by military conscription by whichever administration was in power. However, if they were to follow the rules (especially under Prussian law), they had to apply for permission to leave the country. Naturally they had to apply for a passport which necessitated: a birth certificate which they may or may not have possessed or, at the very least, a christening certificate (also a compulsory deed); a service record from employers (who did not always give these readily); proof that they had sufficient funds (an irony in itself given that this was the most important reason for emigrating), and all men needed to provide proof of completion of obligatory military service. If successful in their application, they then had to make the fact known by announcement in the newspapers and public notices. Needless to say, many young men changed their identity or simply found another way of leaving. This meant, however, that they would not be able to return to their homeland - or at least not without sanctions of some kind. But with yet more political turmoil such as the 1848 uprising, the numbers of emigrants grew to new levels. They were encouraged by advertisements in the papers, mostly from employers established in the developing countries, with offers of work of all kinds and the promise of fortune and the good life.

So it came about that, among those leaving Kirn and Bad Kreuznach in the last half of the l9th century, some descendants of the families whose chronicles have been related were minded to try their skills elsewhere. Valentine the baker made his decision and carried it through and, as has already been mentioned, three of Elise's siblings ventured out to Australia and South America; however, two of her maternal uncles had fetched up in London and through them she also came to London, to be joined later by her sister.

It is now the moment to describe their lives under the emblem of the lion and the unicorn which, due to the quirks of royal descendency, had acquired a German queen and her German prince consort to further the British might throughout the world. This had a great influence on the decision of the emigrants as to where they would see their new lives: overseas with the favourite being north America, or possibly to countries like Canada and Australia where the Victorian influence would also bear weight.

Living with the lion and the unicorn

CHAPTER EIGHT

THE EMIGRANTS

When Josef returned to England with his bride in 1896, his brother Carl had gathered the family to welcome Bertha to her new home - or her home until she and Josef had found their first place to call their own. Elise, their sister-in-law, was beaming, welcoming them warmly and glad to see the usually quiet Josef so happy and loquacious. Young Louise was thrilled to have this new aunt who seemed to be exactly as Josef had described her - warm and at ease, friendly and funny. Charlie was also charmed by her, and baby Elsa, now toddling at eighteen months, wanted to steal the show. The children considered Josef as a second papa, and he did not disappoint, knowing that his Bertha would relish their attachment as well. Carl told them that he and his family wanted to have this first time together just between themselves. He felt that this close relationship was precious as it was the foundation of their new life in England. Josef was very attached to their homeland, but he realised that the stability of their life in England was still not possible in Rhenania. Both he and Carl had very much at heart to contribute their hard work to their country of adoption, to ensure the wellbeing of all of them, but they wanted their children to feel the essence of their background as well.

However, the decision for Uncle Valentine to emigrate from Germany to England, even for economic reasons, was not a simple one and, told to the family over time, his story showed how unprepared he was for this. Once he had broached the subject with his father and found no opposition, his enthusiasm launched him on the road to putting his plan into practice. He went to the authorities to get an emigration passport; he found that it meant losing all rights to German nationality and citizenship. If he wished to live in his homeland again, he would have to pay a not inconsiderable sum of money to do so. This seemed to him to be grossly unfair but he was too proud to go back on his decision. And at 18 years of age he was ready for what he thought would be a great adventure and a life of promise.

THE CHRONICLE OF GEORG VALENTINE HOLZBACHER (1833 - 1919) Part two

Valentine found it quite hard to leave his job in Kreuznach because his widow-employer was quite upset. She had given him an early start to a responsible job and treated him with respect and friendship. He felt sorry for her but thought he must make a future for himself, no matter what. On leaving work for the last time, he went to stay with his father and sister for two weeks, and this was to be the last time he would see his father who died the following year. The railway had not yet reached Bad Kreuznach, so he went by stage coach to the town of Bingen to catch the Rhine steamer to Rotterdam. He had a young lady travelling companion who had been to England once before and was returning, but only for a short visit. On the Rhine steamer passengers were required to stay below deck due to a very severe thunderstorm and torrential rain between Cologne and Emmerich. That part of the journey took four days, and they arrived in Rotterdam on the evening of the fourth day. The next morning Valentine and his fellow passengers caught a steamer to London; this was a freighter with a deck full of cattle. The crossing and travel up the Thames to St. Katharine's Dock took over five days, and Valentine said it was even worse than the journey down the Rhine. Going on deck with the animals was both hazardous and unpleasant, so the travellers stayed below deck which was cramped and stuffy. Valentine was relieved when it was all over.

Valentine's arrival in London happened at the time when German emigration to England was climbing steadily, and migrants found lodging wherever they could, according to their initial means. Employment was not always immediately available and, as early as 1817, a German Benevolent Society had been founded to help those in need. In time other centres were set up to provide assistance. In 1845, through funds raised privately from German sources, a German Hospital was opened in east London. Valentine never said where he went when he stepped foot on English soil but he spent the first month looking for work. His first job was with a baker called Mr. Konraths in Castle Street (near Oxford Street); his wages were five shillings a week. He stayed there for two months and then, tempted by the offer of double his present wages, went to a Mr. Lang in Fore Street in the City.

This was a decision he was to always regret. Although he earned twice his previous wages, the work was three times more. He often worked 20 and 21 hours a day and, when he finally got some rest, his "bedroom" was above the oven and about the same size, reached by a wooden ladder. It was tremendously hot and he told how, when he rose from his bed, he felt giddy and had to take care coming down the ladder. He thought it the most unhealthy place he had ever slept in and, when he compared this to the bakehouse floor in Kreuznach, he preferred the latter! One day he felt so ill that he wanted to find a jobber to do his work for a day so, after he had finished, he walked to the Bakers' Club in Poland Street (Oxford Street) to find someone. There were a number of bakers looking for work but all had heard about the Lang bakery and turned down the offer. He then had to walk back to Fore Street and was so tired that he kept falling asleep. Again and again he would fall against somebody, which would wake him, and then walk on again. It took him a long time but he did get back safely, only to roll up his sleeves and do the usual workload. He began to be sorry he had ever left Germany and sometimes even considered returning to his homeland. However his pride and the belief that he would be thought a coward kept him in England.

One day it was necessary to get in the oven builders for repair work. Work finished earlier than usual and Valentine thought it would be a good opportunity to get some decent sleep. He chose to go down to the coal cellar to get some peace, thinking that his master would otherwise find something for him to do. He spread a flour sack over the coal and managed to sleep for a few hours. That was also a decision he subsequently regretted, for the cellar and the sack were very damp and, a short while later, he had a wheezing sensation in his chest which stayed with him for the rest of his life. This was diagnosed as spasmodic asthma, a very distressing complaint, entirely due to sleeping above the oven in dust and heat. He described how he was young and inexperienced but the job in Fore Street was the worst he ever had. Finally he could stand it no longer and left. He had enough money for very modest board and lodging, but was unemployed for five months. He travelled all over London if he heard of a job vacancy but it was often a fruitless journey. He had to walk such long distances that his shoes wore out and he also injured his ankle. The wound was very large and, as soon as he could, he bought a new pair of boots. Happily his foot healed and never gave him any further trouble.

Finally he succeeded in finding a job with a baker called Mr. Klos on the corner of Great Marlborough Street. He stayed there for a number of years and was earning a top wage of eighteen shillings. So he saved some of that and bought decent clothes. He believed his luck had finally changed for the better. The job suited him better in the type of work he was responsible for. He was never late for the start of work at 10 p.m., finishing the baking at about 7 a.m. He had more opportunity to get out into the fresh air which helped his asthma. Every morning before 8 a.m. he had to deliver the rolls needed by the Palace; this was a permanent order. Whenever they had a ball at the Palace, whilst Prince Albert was still alive, the bakery would supply them with as many as 900 dinner rolls.

It was at this job that Valentine met Ann Brown, the lady who would become his wife. She was English and worked in service further along in Marlborough Street. They were married at St. James Church in Westminster in 1856. On the wedding day Valentine had worked as usual, even serving customers in the early morning, but told no-one what he was going to do later on in the day. He left work as usual during the morning and met his future wife at the church, where they tied the knot with a friend of Ann's, Mrs. Gregory, as witness. After the simple ceremony the three of them went to the pub opposite the church and shared a pint of best bitter - that was their wedding breakfast! After that both Valentine and Ann returned to their work. When Valentine's colleagues found out about the event, one made the couple a wedding cake, another gave them a nice teapot, and the foreman gave them a present of carving knife, fork and steel.

Just when it seemed that things were looking up for Valentine, with a wife he loved to share his life and a job with responsibility that he enjoyed, three months after the wedding his employer died. Having now some savings Valentine decided the time had come to acquire his own business. This was to be another time in his life when the experience he acquired proved to be very costly. He spent three months travelling all over London, following up opportunities that had come to his attention. The first was with a friend who offered to sell Valentine his shop in Walworth. However, when it came to proceeding with the purchase, his friend withdrew the offer and, as Valentine had nothing in writing, he learnt the hard lesson that business and friendship are not good bed-fellows. The second shop was in Woolwich and looked promising, so Valentine paid a £5.- deposit to secure the purchase. However, this subsequently fell through because, although the business rightfully belonged to a widow, she had no legal right to sell it as her husband had omitted to make a will. The widow would not reimburse Valentine and, although he could have got his £5.- back by going to the law courts, he had no desire to go to such lengths. So he lost quite a sum of money which he could well have done with not long after.

Finally he settled on the third choice, a business situated in West Street in north Bermondsey. Such purchases were always different and fraught with complications. The price of the bakery was £80.-, a not inconsiderable sum of money, but this did not include the lease. So the owner made it available on an arrangement which would best be described as hire/purchase. Valentine had to achieve a level of turnover each week on which his weekly payment was based. The level was higher than he could manage at the beginning, and so it was a hard struggle for him and his wife to make ends meet. The customer base was almost half to credit customers, which Valentine was obliged to respect. However, when he saw that a number of them were taking advantage not to meet their debt, he gradually turned them away. Once again he realised that others were not as honest as he always was, and the experience cost the couple dearly for many months.

Valentine and his wife worked very hard and finally, at the end of the first year, the business started to produce results. The lease payments were finished; Valentine was able to produce more, baking Sunday dinners as well for a while. Ann had no domestic help but did the housework herself as well as serving behind the counter. Valentine took on one employee to lessen the stress, but he was still on his feet from 2 a.m. to

10 p.m. His feet would swell up and he was thoroughly exhausted. Ann wanted him to rest but, if he fell asleep, she had enormous trouble rousing him. With such swollen feet, she made him soak them in hot water before continuing his work.

Nevertheless, the couple enjoyed their years in West Street, living above the shop and making new friends. During this time Valentine's brother Carl Christian came to visit him for two weeks. He also had experienced a terrible sea crossing and thought his time had come - but happily he was mistaken and his fear of never seeing his wife and sons again became groundless. Valentine also became friendly with the German manager of another bakery nearby; this led to a friendship between the men and their wives which lasted for many years. When both couples had sold their businesses and retired, they went travelling together, visiting their homeland and also other European countries.

In 1861 Valentine bought another business in Jamaica Road, Bermondsey, which was in a better position and did twice the trade. He was becoming much more astute in his business activities and was buying flour on a larger scale, as much as 1,400 sacks at a time. This naturally meant getting more advantageous prices on his raw materials, thus increasing the profit margins of his shops. In 1868 he bought yet another bakery in Red Lion Street, Holborn, selling the Jamaica Road business to his German friend. Valentine and Ann went to live over the shop in Holborn and it was even more profitable, but they did not like the house or the neighbourhood. The same was true of his friend who did not really like Jamaica Road, so they made an exchange, and Valentine and Ann moved back to Jamaica Road where they stayed for another 8 years.

Valentine said that he heard some people remark that he and Ann had made their money easily. He thought that they might change their minds if they experienced the hard work the couple had done in the twenty and more years of running their own businesses. Valentine had become a good businessman and invested wisely in the trade he knew so well. However, the injury to health was great, and all bakers almost inevitably suffered from some form of lung disease due to the flour dust, steam from the bread, smoke from the coal, and the heat of the furnaces and ovens. This was the case for Valentine whose health had worsened considerably, and so the couple took the decision to sell their profitable businesses and did so in the spring of 1877. They decided to get out of the London air for that coming summer and went three months to Germany. However, Valentine found his problems were almost worse and was so ill that a doctor had to be called. It was thought he might die but he eventually recovered.

His brother Carl Christian had died in 1870, and so there was just one sister left who, at the time of Valentine's visit, was extremely poorly.

Carl Christian's wife received a small widow's pension from the German post office; his eldest son Carl Josef was finishing his last year of commercial training, the second son (also called Valentine) was a baker's apprentice but unreliable, and the last son Josef was still at school being ten years old. Valentine and Ann convinced sister Christina to go to England with them, so that they could look after her properly. He talked at length to nephew Carl and asked him to think about coming to London when he finished his apprenticeship; Valentine thought the young man's chances were far more promising in England, especially as he was particularly gifted with languages.

When they returned to London, Valentine purchased two houses in Naylor Road, Peckham. In the October of the same year they moved into one of them, together with Valentine's sister Christina. Unfortunately Christina's health had deteriorated even further and she died soon after. So Valentine found himself bereft of immediately family, except for his three nephews in Kreuznach. The eldest Carl Josef had meanwhile finished his commercial training; he had listened to his Uncle Valentine's advice and decided it was right for him to forge a career for himself in London. Carl's mother Regine was very sad to see him go but saw the wisdom of his decision, and she gave him her blessing. She was to die not long afterwards. Carl's brother Valentine seemed unable to settle and decided to go out to Australia where he found work as a baker in Sydney. That left young Josef who, at 14, still had to continue his education. A family by the name of Maurer had been very kind to the widowed Regine when she found life difficult and they took in Josef when she died. The Maurers, as we have seen in the chronicles, were distantly related, and they looked after Josef until his professional training finished in 1886.

Valentine and Ann took advantage of their freedom to take extended holidays, both in England by the sea and by travelling back to Germany with their friends visiting new places in their homeland that they had never seen. Another year they went even further afield into Switzerland where they were thrilled by the lakes and snow-capped mountains of the central regions, finishing with the Rhine waterfalls and the lake of Constance. After the unification of the various Germanic states, dominated by Prussia, in 1871, the new Germany became more affluent, developing industries and railways. Valentine remarked that they experienced very pleasant trips but found everything had become very expensive. He observed that the waiters in the hotels were like sharks: "no matter what you give them, they are always looking for more"!

Valentine's health problems continued to plague him and, at one stage, he was near to death and was bed-bound for many months. He and Ann were very religious people, and Valentine never ceased to be amazed at his advancing age. He believed that they had been looked upon kindly by the almighty, and were happy to enjoy each day that brought no problems. The couple celebrated their 40th wedding anniversary in style, surrounded by all their nearest family in London.

-0-0-0-0-0-0-0-0-0-0-0-

Carl and his family were at breakfast. They were discussing all the events which had been planned for Queen Victoria's Diamond Jubilee.

"Was there ever another king or queen who reigned for sixty years?" asked Louise.

"Not as far as I know", answered her father. "Most people don't live to become that old".

"Illa told me her aunt Julia lived to be eighty-four years old", put in Josef. "That's older than the Queen is now".

"Are we going to see the parade?" asked Charlie.

The adults looked at each other, questioningly. Elise had just given birth to another baby daughter Margaret, whom they all called Maggie, and little Elsa was only just three years old. The two older children looked at their parents expectantly.

"Well", replied Carl. "We'll see nearer the time. It's supposed to be on the 22nd June, so we still have time to think about it. Right now my thoughts would be that it is too much for your mama, with your new baby sister to look after; Elsa is too small to enjoy it and she would get tired very quickly. She would probably be rather frightened of the big crowds which will no doubt be there".

The children looked crestfallen. Then their new aunt Bertha had another idea.

"Why don't we make it into our own celebration? We can have a big party in the garden and invite all the family and maybe some of our best friends".

Everyone spoke at the same time but they all thought it was a marvellous idea, and probably much more enjoyable than being in the crowds and probably not seeing very much. With the promise of a party Louise and Charlie cheered up and asked when it would be.

"It is a very good idea", said Josef. "We must make it a real celebration of our good fortune in having so many members of the family nearby. Personally I shall always be sorry it is not in our beautiful homeland, between the Rhine and the hills and valleys of the Moselle and the Nahe. Having said that, I know how fortunate we are to be here enjoying peace and many good things".

Carl added: "Well, yes, and I have grown quite attached to England which has been so welcoming to us Germans. Maybe we do have the influence of Victoria and Albert to thank for some of that, but I find the English people are mostly very friendly. We work hard, I agree, but we do get the rewards and can make plans without wondering whether we are going to be subjected to more upheaval".

"It would seem that, since the unification under Bismarck and with the new Kaiser, Germany is becoming more stable and affluent on the whole", said Bertha. "At least we can go back for holidays and see how those of the family who have survived the changes are getting on. By the way, my sister will be coming on a visit in a few weeks' time, and we shall hear more from her about things in Frankfurt, for example".

And so the discussion went on for quite some time. A date for the party was suggested, and it was thought that Louise and Charlie could help greatly by making the invitations with specially painted cards all individually inscribed inside. Louise had quite good artistic talents and loved drawing, and Charlie had good handwriting - a combination which suited them both. It must be said that most members of the family had a talent in one or another way, and they derived much joy from handcrafts, cooking and making music in particular.

Some time went by, and the family was enjoying the break for Easter. Louise and Charlie were on holiday from school and had finished the invitation cards which were being addressed to send out. Louise was looking at the list of guests and thought how nice it was to have such a lot of relatives.

"Mama, what a shame your father is not there to see us all. Would he have been pleased?"

Elise looked at her much loved eldest daughter. "I have never spoken much about your grandfather, have I?"

Charlie and Louise begged their mother to tell them about her young days growing up in Kirn.

CHAPTER NINE

ELISE TELLS HER STORY

"Well, children, your grandfather Wilhelm Reichardt was a polisher of agate, which is a form of quartz quarried near our town. The Kirn agate is a beautiful golden brown and black, and was highly prized for quite a while. He married our mother Maria Turck when he was twenty-one years old; she was five years older but she was very pretty, and very astute when it came to business. When the agate polishing was bringing in good money, she helped Wilhelm to purchase two houses in the Neue Strasse, which had just been built on the edge of the old town. She showed him how to get a more advantageous price if he bought two houses at the same time. Although it was a substantial outlay at the beginning, the family could live in one and the other house could be rented out to bring in an income. In the 1850s the Jewish population increased after a long absence from Kirn, and Wilhelm rented the second house to a Jewish family named Rothschild. So there was always some income when the agate polishing slowed down. For a time our father made the long stems for tobacco pipes but this did not last either.

"Our mother bore four children in six years - my eldest brother Wilhelm who went to Fiji and is now in Australia, my brother Julius who accompanied me to England and then went out to Uruguay where he lives with his family, myself Elisabeth, and my sister Louise who is here also. My mother died in childbirth with our youngest brother Louis in 1863; he also went to Australia. Obviously her death was terrible for my father. For a while we little ones were cared for by our grandmother Turck; she was very kind to us but we were a lot for her to look after. Some time later father took a second wife who was very nice to us as well, but she also gave him four more children, of whom I only know my half-brother Christian who is also here in England now, Jean who is a professional soldier in the Prussian army, and the last two who have not given us news since my father's death.

"You know your uncles John Turck and his brother Philipp who have lived here in London for quite a few years now. Uncle John first went out to Australia where he married an English lady and had two children. However, his wife wanted to return to England, and so the family came back and - as you know - they ran a bakery, just like Uncle Valentine used to. Uncle Philipp worked in a bank in London, and he was the one who suggested to my father that I should come here also. He found a place for me as lady's companion to a Scottish lady called Miss Wemyss.

"That is how, when I was seventeen years old, Julius and I set out for London. Like your father we also took a steamer down the Rhine to Rotterdam where we secured a passage on a freight ship. There was a storm while we were crossing the sea, and the ship developed a leak. Julius was called upon to help man the pumps, and I was put ready into a lifeboat with some of my belongings, alongside some other women and children. We were given tea and biscuits from time to time but we were not put into the water. We may well have perished at sea but, after what seemed to be a very long time, another ship took us in tow and, slowly but surely, the two ships made their way up the Thames estuary to dock in London. There we heard we had been given up for lost at sea and thought to be dead. But all I lost was a few belongings; I thought it had been a great adventure and that sea crossings were always like that!

"While I was with Miss Wemyss I visited my uncles a lot, and that is how I met you father - when he found work in Crouch End in north London, it was too far to travel daily from Peckham, and he took a room in Islington. This is where we all went to the German church, and where we met and knew we would spend our lives together. We started our married life in Crouch End but, after you were born, the lodgings were too small. Your father found a house in Marquis Road, where we now all live and where your brother and sisters have been born. Our only sorrow here has been the loss of your baby brother Otto Philipp in 1889, but our otherwise happy life has helped to heal the wounds".

-0-0-0-0-0-0-0-0-0-0-0-

"Mama", said Louise as Elise finished her story. "I am nearly thirteen...."

"No, my lovely, you are only just twelve!"

"Well, yes. But I wondered, before I get much older, if I could go with Uncle Josef and Aunt Bertha when they go next time to Germany. I would so love to meet the people we know in Kirn and Bad Kreuznach".

Elise smiled. "Get much older…? You are not a grandmother yet, you know! But yes, I expect your papa would even quite like you to see the places we talk about and the people, or those who are still there".

CHAPTER TEN

CELEBRATION AND THANKSGIVING

Thus it happened that 1897 was not just a year to celebrate Victoria's sixty years as Queen of England, Ireland, Scotland and Wales, and Empress of India, sovereign of the British Empire. Lesser mortals from Germany were also celebrating many years of living in England where, with their hard work and dedication, they had been able to make a peaceful and stable life for their families. As planned, Carl and Elise welcomed to the party twelve other members of their respective families, together with eight children - two born in Australia and all the others in London. They had intended to invite some of their good English friends but found that, with already twenty-two people in just the immediate family, their house and garden was already filled to capacity. In that number was a most unusual visitor: Carl and Josef's brother Valentine who had returned unannounced from Australia.

They were not alone in giving thanks for their good fortune. The decades of prosperity which came through global trading and the seemingly endless resources of the places colonised by the British had brought about gradual improvements in the lives of even the nation's poorest people. This was not necessarily altruistic, although a good deal was initiated by affluent members of the Quaker movement. One of the best examples of this was the new village of Bournville being built by the Cadburys the chocolate manufacturers, but it had become a trend for industrialists to provide better living conditions for their workers. After all, they needed healthy workers to produce their wealth. Even in the east end of London, there were socialist movements actively promoting and obtaining better basic education for working class children.

So in their own way Carl and Elise, and all the allied relatives, expressed their gratitude for the goodness in their lives. They were all fluent in English, both written and spoken - although one or two still had very recognisable accents. The children, on the other hand, spoke to each other then and later always in English. They went to English schools but also learnt their parents' mother tongue not just in their homes but also through the German church community. The two English members of the family, Uncle Valentine's wife Ann and Uncle John's wife Catherine, completed the balance of the two cultures.

The ensuing years brought no particularly unpleasant occurrences. However, there was a gradually noticeable change in the politics of both Britain and Germany. Then, in the late 1890s and very early 20th century Britain engaged in its first major conflict since the Crimean war in 1859. The Boer war in South Africa was particularly nasty in that it affected civilian populations more than before. It was where the idea of concentration camps was first put into practice by the British.

The death of Queen Victoria in 1901 can be said to have sealed the fate of what was to come for, although she had become less able as she lived into old age, her influence was still apparent. The Crown Prince of Wales came to the throne as Edward VII and gave a very different flavour to the monarchy. His mother had reigned for so long and had excluded him from the work of the sovereign that he had become a leisure-loving playboy. In Germany, meanwhile, Wilhelm II had become Kaiser and dispensed with the services of Bismarck. Wilhelm was ruthlessly ambitious, violently jealous of the British Empire, and hated his uncle Edward VII. He pushed Germany to acquire more colonies, and went all out to make the German navy more powerful than that of Great Britain.

Thus, as the new century gained momentum, the Germans who had been living in England for decades and felt so much at home became increasingly anxious about this rivalry between the cousins. Furthermore, the British monarchy had very good relations with their cousin the Russian Tsar Nicholas, and even made a political agreement in 1905 to the exclusion of the German cousin (second cousin only to Nicholas).

This worrying situation provoked many discussions in the Holzbacher and Reichardt families about their situation in Britain. There was no real reason during the first years of the Edwardian reign to fear any disruption of their livelihoods. However, John Turck and Christian

Reichardt both decided to proceed with naturalisation, thus acquisition of British nationality. Uncle Valentine, on the other hand, remained staunchly by his belief that where a person was born, where their genes and their blood came from, that was the essence of their being; no change of paper documents would ever alter what somebody truly was. Ann, his English wife, respected his views and thought that, in any case, she was English and that this was their safeguard - which they did not believe would be necessary in any case. Carl trusted what he perceived as the honesty and fairness of the English people, as had been his experience of the last two decades and more. His children were British-born. He was not so naive that he thought nothing could ever change, but he was of the opinion that he could adapt well enough to any new requirements. Josef did not get involved in these discussions; privately he believed that, if he and Bertha were to be a burden on Carl in the business or otherwise, they could return to Germany where he would doubtless find employment in the improved conditions there.

During this first decade of the 20th century, Uncle Valentine and Aunt Ann celebrated their golden wedding, and Carl and Elise their thirtieth anniversary, Christian Reichardt had married another Bertha from the German community and three little boys had made their appearance. In 1907 young Louise, now a beautiful twenty-one year old, met Otto Fricke, a young German who had also found his way to the German church in

Islington. Otto was a young entrepreneurial salesman who was always on the lookout for opportunities - and there were plenty of those. He was a restless man, settling for a while and then finding an opening to go off somewhere. Louise was deeply in love and she soon came to realise that she was the one who would have to adapt the most. She knew he was a maverick and that it would be no good to try and restrain his independent nature. They married in 1910, with Louise's father Carl providing the best wedding he knew how. She quickly bore Otto four boys, although he was often away for weeks and months at a time. It seemed that he nevertheless provided a good home for his young family, wherever he was.

At the turn of the century young Charlie was finishing his education, both in England and Germany, and then went into his father's business. Carl's employer and owner of the business had retired, and Carl had bought the business from him. With their language skills and now considerable experience in the purchase and sale of essential oils, Carl - together with his brother Josef and son Charlie - continued to make a good living for them all, operating from an office and warehouse just a few yards from the Thames in the city of London. Carl's second daughter Elsa later finished her education and trained in office skills, and she happily joined the family business dealing with all the correspondence (English, German and even French at her father's dictation). Although a naturally quiet young person, she was very intelligent and enjoyed being out in the world. Perhaps Elsa was less attached to the German way of life than her older siblings, although she also enjoyed that side of her life. She knew she was pure German but felt completely at home with the British way of life.

In early 1913 Elsa gave the family a huge shock when she was stricken very suddenly with a burst appendix and peritonitis. Her parents immediately called the doctor; he came very quickly and advised them that she was in danger of losing her life. He told them there was no time to get her to hospital, and that she would not survive the journey. With the surgical skills all doctors of the times were obliged to have, he swiftly organised for the kitchen table to be prepared, on which he would do the operation. He also immediately sent for a nurse who would act as anaesthetist, administering chloroform under his instruction. Elise was his assistant for all else, providing the large quantities of hot water needed for the instruments and towels and rags, indeed everything which he would need for cleanliness. Thus Elsa's life hung in the balance but, thanks to the rapid intervention and obvious magnificent skills of the doctor, she survived the ordeal. It took many months of nursing care until she was fully recovered; she was made to eat raw liver and watercress to compensate for the blood loss, and had a huge scar right across her abdomen. But she was alive and, for that, her parents were hugely grateful.

Also in 1913 Uncle Valentine had to bear the loss of his beloved wife Ann. Although for years he had repeatedly said how grateful they both were to have been able to enjoy the years of retirement, he was now also in his eightieth year and becoming very fragile. Despite his deep spiritual beliefs he became bewildered and gradually began losing his mind. The family rallied round but he was like a lost soul.

Another event in 1913 was the marriage of Charlie with a German lady, Margarethe, who was a good friend of his sister Louise and whom they had met at the German church in Islington.

-0-0-0-0-0-0-0-0-0-0-0-

Christmas 1913 saw the family gathered together again, somewhat battered and bruised, and in a much quieter mood. These days they were increasingly keeping to themselves because of the growing tension and rise of bad feeling towards foreigners. For once Otto Fricke was spending more time with his young family, now counting two little sons and another baby to be born in two months' time. So, whilst Carl and Elise now had grandchildren to enjoy, they felt a lot less secure. Carl was more prone to becoming very anxious and it took Elise much more effort to convince him that, as long as they were all together, they would get through any difficulties.

Christmas turned into New Year and, in February 1914, Louise had yet another little boy they named Willi. Otto was again off travelling, and Louise found a young country girl to live in and help with all the work created by three very young children. Although she usually managed with all her household chores on her own, she was finding that a young family needed a lot of energy, especially when the babies came so quickly in succession. She also had noticed that people's friendliness and readiness to help was no longer so forthcoming. She always spoke English to her little son Carl, now three, and to her other little boys as they grew. However, it was known that Otto was German, and what had been the odd rumbling complaint before about Germans in particular was now becoming louder and more aggressive.

One Sunday, Louise left the baby with the maid and took the two older boys to see their grandparents. Elsa opened the door to her much loved elder sister and little nephews.

"How wonderful to see you up and looking much better these days", said Louise.

"I am indeed, Louise. And I have been back to work with Papa three days a week. It is so good to be doing things again, and not feeling so tired any more. But you will find Papa very anxious - I have to warn you - and Mama and Uncle Josef are hard put to reassure him", replied Elsa.

Carl and Elise were delighted to see their eldest daughter and exclaimed how much the little boys had grown. They greeted their grandsons in German, quite naturally, and were surprised when young Carl spoke his greeting pointedly in English. They had not really thought about it because, when with their own children, they had always spoken a lot of German but also unfailingly reverted to English when Aunt Ann or sister-in-law Catherine came to visit. They considered it a matter of common courtesy and, in any case, they passed easily from one language into the other. But there was an awkward silence when Carl said his "Good afternoon". To change the mood, Elsa said to the boys: "Come with me, boys. Uncle Charlie found his wooden toys the other day in the attic, and he brought them downstairs for you to play with when you come to see us". The little fellows eagerly went with their auntie to play with the farmyard animals which had given so many hours of pleasure to their uncle when he was small.

As Elsa well knew, once the children were happily playing elsewhere, her parents and Louise would be able to talk without constraint.

"Louise", said Carl hesitantly. "You know I would not interfere in your life, but your mama and I get so worried these days when Otto is not there with you. Would it not be a good thing if Elsa came to stay with you for a while?"

"Papa, I can understand your concern. And I have realised since 1905, when the new Aliens Act was brought in, that being a German might have its drawbacks. Otto is, of course, of German descent and nationality, which means the children and I have also acquired German nationality, but I am British-born, as are the children. This cannot be ignored, surely?"

"I hope not, I sincerely hope not, but people have changed so much towards us. It is as if we have become outcasts, and I cannot understand what we have done wrong".

Elise chipped in: "I keep trying to tell your papa that it is political, and that it is because the royal cousins are almost at each other's throats. Kaiser Wilhelm just cannot accept what King George has, it is dreadful. Why do our countries need to compete - we both should be enjoying the prosperity".

"I agree, Mama" said Louise. "But since he was made a partner and is practically running the business for his employer, Otto feels that his work is not in danger at present. As you know, he has brought some lucrative business from the chocolate manufacturers - all of them, not just Cadbury's but also Rowntree and Fry. The advertising material is also liked by the soap manufacturers, and he has built up good relations with Unilever. He is very optimistic about it all".

Carl looked thoughtfully at his daughter. Above all, he did not want to dampen her spirits. However, like his own business and that of his brother-in-law Christian who dealt in oriental china and porcelain, Otto's business relied heavily on imports, and Carl saw complications looming if the tension between Germany and Britain were to worsen. He remembered all the discussions that had taken place between different family members about the question of naturalisation. He knew that his brother-in-law Christian had taken the step in 1905 when the Aliens Act was passed, but he was among those who could not see that it was necessary. He realised now that he may have been wrong in his assessment of the future but still hoped for the best.

The following week he had a long conversation with Josef about their family business. They both agreed to make an immediate investment in raw materials from abroad, just in case such purchases were to get more difficult. They were prudent businessmen and had made savings both for their business and separately for their private purposes. So they considered themselves to be in the best possible position at this stage and felt that they should be able to cope with any difficulties that might arise. Thus, in those early months of 1914, the families carried on as usual, living quietly and going about their lives perhaps somewhat more unobtrusively so as to avoid any provocation so easily aroused by the simple fact of their origin.

Never to spare the family's concerns for him, Louise's husband Otto went off to Germany despite their fear that he might not be able to return. Official papers were becoming not just indispensable but difficult to obtain, especially when it concerned dealings with Germany; every detail had to be explained and justified. Otto was a very secretive person and Carl, in particular, privately worried about Otto's activities. Louise's faith in her husband was unshakeable and, in any case, Carl and Elise were very careful to hide their worry for her. They were also anxious about their own last child and third daughter Maggie who was just seventeen. She was always a moody girl, preferring her own company, and recently she was almost refusing to go out saying she had many books to read in her room. Elsa and Maggie were very different and, if the truth be known, did not get on very well. Elsa was very attached to her elder sister Louise but Maggie appeared detached from them all. Carl and Elise thought that this had become worse and that she might have been the object of some of the verbal abuse being thrown at Germans. However, she would not talk about anything and maintained she was absolutely fine, just wanted to be on her own.

With Carl taking care of the family business and general family matters, Josef had taken on the responsibility of helping Uncle Valentine. He had done his best to accompany him through the difficult time of the Ann's funeral, and he was extremely sensitive to his uncle's disorientation. Josef was beginning to fear that it was not just bereavement and grief which was affecting Valentine's mental state. He took advantage of the better moments to make sure that his uncle's wishes were known and specified as to what should happen whenever he also passed on. Uncle Valentine said immediately after Ann's funeral that he wished to be buried at her side, and so the plot was purchased in the cemetery only a month after her demise. More difficult was the question of his last will and testament, and this took some time. It was finally done to Valentine's satisfaction, and he wished to leave his not inconsiderable estate to his nephews Carl and Josef, with Christian Reichardt as executor. The latter arrangement was not just necessary but also wise, since Christian had British nationality and the others did not.

Finally there were Elise's relatives, including uncles John and Philipp Turck and family. In the middle of the first decade they had felt the necessity to re-connect with their homeland. Philipp had not married, and his brother John and wife Catherine went with him to Germany, accompanied by their daughter Ellen. Their son Louis was much involved in business in London, and did not go with them. Whilst there Ellen met a young German and married him, so her parents and uncle decided they would stay in Germany. Louis looked after their interests in England during their absence. Elise's sister Louie and her husband Stephen Gourmer took on a hotel in Islington in 1906, and were also feeling vulnerable. Their children, now young adults also, stayed with them and helped in the business.

Conflict as never before

CHAPTER ELEVEN

HOW SO FEW CAN DESTROY SO MANY

Hardly more than a decade before, people in Britain were finding more opportunities than ever and could not have imagined how their lives would be shattered irretrievably. Nor would they have even suspected how insidiously and cruelly this was brought about by leaders, political and royal, and the press. Britain liked to present itself as open-minded, fair and welcoming; in the years prior to the declaration of war in 1914 this assertion would also be shattered. Political alliances had been made over the preceding years so that, when Archduke Ferdinand was assassinated in Sarajevo, each nation had to take up position with those it had aligned with. In August 1914 the grand empires were at war, with hatred and arrogance leading to such confrontation as never seen before.

The very next day after the declaration a new Aliens Restriction Act was rushed through the British parliament with very little dissent. Foreign residents were subjected to a level of parliamentary attention, public controversy and press coverage totally disproportionate to the numbers concerned. It was xenophobia and extremist prejudice to an unprecedented degree.

While British young men rushed in their droves to enlist in the army or navy, it was with fear and trepidation that Carl and Elise, Josef and Bertha, Louie and Stephen, Uncle Valentine and Otto Fricke obeyed the order to register with the police for residence permits. This was to be followed by other measures according to their individual status. Because this Act had been brought in so swiftly, and then followed by an even more virulent Defence of the Realm Act, there was confusion for weeks as to the criteria for each case. Carl and his relatives accepted the need for these measures - after all, their forebears and, to some degree, they themselves had been obliged to do similar things in their very homeland. What was harder to understand was the intemperate abuse and occasional violence being shown towards them, in particular as Germans - now considered to be responsible for the war and almost certainly spies. The first distinction to be made by the authorities was 'Enemy Aliens' from the Central Powers - which were the German, Austro-Hungarian and Ottoman empires and also the Kingdom of Bulgaria, and then 'Friendly Aliens' which were those from other nations who were allies or basically not involved.

Over the next weeks and months the restrictions started to affect Carl and Josef and the others. Initially, while their cases were under consideration, they were restricted as to where they lived. They had to demonstrate a good knowledge of English, not a problem for any of them, and also demonstrate that they were of good character, again not a problem. They were not allowed to travel more than five miles from their home and a curfew was imposed. In early 1915 things really took a turn for the worse as Carl's business was confiscated and shut down. This meant that the family had to rely on their savings. When the businesses of enemy alien owners were liquidated, a portion of the realised assets went to government appointed "custodians". The remainder of the proceeds, after payment of all debts and other expenses due from the business, was in theory distributed among non-enemy shareholders and/or others with a financial entitlement. The only non-alien associate in Carl's business was his son Charlie who was British-born. However, due to the nature of the business which relied on imports, the only proceeds which could be saved in these conditions came from the value of the stock. Confusion continued to reign and bad will even more so, and financially the families all had to be very careful with what they had managed to save.

Originally everyone thought the war would be finished within six months, but this was far from the case and the casualties - both killed and wounded - began to take on huge proportions. Germans were blamed even more vehemently and, after the sinking of the Lusitania, hatred rose to fever pitch. In the spring of 1915, the measures taken against German aliens in particular were stepped up. This was when the destinies of Carl and the whole family were set in motion. Josef was of military age - only just but enough for the authorities - so he was interned, firstly in London and then for almost three years at one of the main internment camps on the Isle of Man called Knockaloe. His beloved wife Bertha was among the 20,000 mainly women and children who were repatriated to their homeland, there to fend for themselves; having been out of their country for so many years, quite a few had nowhere to go but Bertha still had family in Frankfurt am Main where she could stay. She and Josef could correspond sporadically, whenever allowed, but Josef felt very isolated and they both suffered greatly from being separated so far from each other, and they knew not for how long.

Carl's daughter Louise and her small boys were British-born but had German nationality through their father, so they were registered but not restricted, except possibly financially. Her husband Otto, on the other hand, was interned for the next three years. He had claimed to be exempt from internment since he had, according to his own account only, helped a British officer named Montgomery at the beginning of the war. Whether this was so or not, he was fortunate enough to be detained in a small internment camp in Islington, north London, and so Louise was able to visit him as much as was allowed. Internment for Otto was a real trial; he had a restless nature and being confined indefinitely was his worst nightmare. However, the prisoners were not badly treated, so he set about "organising" the camp and in time convinced the camp administrator to allow the internees to take charge of their own budget. The building they occupied was a former workhouse, so there were catering and laundry facilities they could use. They organised themselves according to their skills and, even if they were charged more for their supplies, they were allowed to make their own purchases from those delivering to the camp. Their diet was not very varied but better than many.

Louise had given birth to a fourth child in January 1916, but she still faithfully visited Otto if possible once a week and took some food - usually preserved in one way or another - although she probably did not have masses for her growing family either. Some of the internees had private funds which they could still lay their hands on, and others with artisan skills made objects from materials found or brought in by relatives. If possible these articles were sold and brought in a little cash.

Carl and Elise were devastated when Josef and Bertha had to leave, but their ordeal was to become worse. The increase in patriotic hysteria and bad feelings towards Germans, together with economic pressures, meant that they were obliged to leave their home of nearly thirty years. Their two youngest daughters were still at home, Maggie now eighteen and Elsa twenty-one - so technically of age. Carl applied for exemption from repatriation; theoretically he fulfilled several of the criteria, such as residence in Britain for at least thirty-five years and with three or more British subjects as sponsors. However, with his father now nearly sixty years old, son Charlie felt he needed to give his father the biggest chance of exemption by joining the British army. This would also benefit his wife who had acquired British nationality when they married but was still considered as enemy alien. It was the act which gave the most weight in such circumstances, but for Carl it was the worst of all conditions. In the summer of 1916 Charlie was put in the Middlesex Regiment which set up eight infantry labour companies for the British-born sons of enemy alien parentage. At the same time he also took the step of adding the English name of Holt to his surname, which he announced to be his last and principal surname - added, however, to the surname of Holzbacher. He announced this from the office where his father's business had been in operation and from his residence in north London. Thus he had been able to keep the office if not the business, and he could offer shelter to his parents when they had become homeless.

As to Uncle Valentine, now an ageing widower, it fell to Elise's brother Christian to see that he was properly looked after. Apart from Charlie, Christian was the only one of the close family who was able to travel around without restriction - how wise he had been to naturalise in 1905; he also assumed and adopted by deed poll the English name of Hayter but, like Charlie, it was added to his German surname Reichardt. His business could no longer function as imports from China and Japan became problematic if not impossible. However, Christian had also wisely invested in one or two properties from which he could, at the very least, draw rent. He saw to Uncle Valentine's care and financial interests as the old man gradually sank into dementia. It also fell to him to offer lodging to Carl and Elise whenever they could not stay elsewhere, and the two girls Elsa and Maggie stayed wherever they could.

When Otto was interned, after some time Louise went to live in one of Christian's properties in north London so that she would be safe from eviction by a prejudiced landlord. Her sister Elsa would stay to help her from time to time. Now able to decide on her own path, Elsa would not rest at home and eventually found herself a typist's job with a pacifist organisation which set up office in London in 1916. Through these peace-loving, open-minded and courageous people, Elsa and her family found British people who treated them as equals. It was a great comfort, and the family had nothing but admiration for the work of this association, even though it was having only a limited effect.

As more months and years passed the emotional and mental agony of these enemy alien families became immersed in the now immensely devastating effects of this most terrible of wars. For the first time in British history the civilian population was targeted in their homes not just by the new advent of air raids by Zeppelin bombing, but also by food rationing and shortages, by the obligation of military conscription for all men between the ages of eighteen and forty-one, by the relentless propaganda from the government and the press, and even by the restrictions imposed by the wide-ranging powers of the Defence of the Realm Act. Under the latter anyone could be court-martialled for loitering under railway bridges, feeding wild animals, discussing naval or military affairs, and quite a few other such activities normally without suspicion. A whole generation of young men was being decimated or deeply wounded physically and mentally. Not just in Britain but even more all over Europe and further afield, the scale of destruction of places and people was without precedent. Unreasoning hatred was rife; all nature of human suffering was inflicted on people of all kinds; animals were slaughtered in their millions either through military use or to feed primarily troops and, if they were lucky, civilian populations.

As the fighting continued inexorably until, in 1918, a very uneasy armistice was reached, the various members of the alien families awaited the solutions to be imposed on their lives. Even before the armistice was signed, the German internees numbering over 25,000 were gradually being repatriated. Otto Fricke took advantage of an opportunity to be included in those being shipped to camps in Holland. After some time the internees were told that their wives could join them, and Otto urged Louise to do so. Her problem was that children could not go as well, and she was never going to leave her little boys behind. Such was the pressure from Otto that Louise moved heaven and earth to be allowed to take the children with her; she was finally successful and regretfully left behind her parents and siblings, and indeed the life she had nevertheless enjoyed. She sold all her furniture to pay for their passage and, in October 1918, with her boys aged from two to nearly eight years, travelled via Harwich and Rotterdam to a camp in Zwolle; the whole journey took three days because of the chaotic transport conditions.

They were hardly settled when the armistice was signed, and all the German families were told they were being repatriated. They were put on to trains, destination unknown, often shunted on to sidings which, in fact, was sometimes a blessing for it provided an opportunity to get the children out in the air and see to their needs. They were on the train for days and arrived at a station just over the border in Germany. They were then split up; Louise and the three youngest boys were sent to a school where they were given a badly needed warm meal and straw mattresses to sleep on. Otto and eldest son Carl stayed in nearby barracks. They were then gradually all processed and given travel documents for the next stage of the journey.

Suddenly they heard someone shouting their name and, joy of joys, saw Josef who was also being repatriated. He was on his way to Frankfurt am Main where his beloved wife Bertha was eagerly awaiting his arrival. Louise, Otto and the children travelled to Cologne where Otto originally hoped to get established. However, they were not allowed to leave the station because of ongoing military operations, and so decided to continue and try to reach Bad Kreuznach or Kirn where Louise had family. It was no easy journey with rail transport in disarray but they finally arrived in Kirn, where they were given a warm welcome by relatives.

In England, once the armistice had been signed, Carl and Elise were still dependent on their relatives for somewhere to stay. When Louise left, they moved into the house where she had been living and which belonged to Elise's brother Christian. Charlie was demobbed, with the service medals given to those who served, and was trying to piece his life back together. Maggie had now also come of age, and so Carl and Elise were certain to be repatriated.

In 1919, through the work of the organisation employing her, Elsa met an Englishman who had just spent almost three years in prison as a conscientious objector. The couple fell in love, she was 26 years and he almost 30 years old. Elsa brought Ted home to meet her parents who felt the couple to be suited and approved the engagement. Carl was desolate that he had no money to finance his second daughter's wedding or help them to get established. He was suffering from bouts of severe depression, still not understanding why he had been made to feel like a criminal. He had no rights and still had to apply periodically for exemption from repatriation. Uncle Valentine had passed away earlier that same year, but the British government did not allow Carl or Josef to receive their inheritance - they were still enemy aliens in official eyes. As Christian Reichardt had been designated executor, he was authorised to receive the legacy once the heavy taxes had been levied and probate granted.

In 1920 Elsa married her Englishman, after which Carl and Elise were finally shipped off to Germany. They settled in a place on the Rhine not far from Cologne where Otto and Louise had found a new life after a couple of short business ventures. Youngest daughter Maggie went with them - her brother Charlie and sister Elsa were married, and so she opted to accompany her parents. She had met an Englishman of the Quaker faith, who had also been a conscientious objector but for less time than Ted and not in prison but on a farm. His name was Eric, and he was to find training and employment with the German company Scholl, so he went to Germany as well. Maggie and Eric married and their first child, a son Alan, was born there. Some time later, Eric was transferred back to England soon after to work with Scholl in London. This meant that Carl and Elise were feeling more and more isolated and, in the mid-1920s they had virtually no family within easy reach.

As Christian Reichardt was a British subject, he carried on living in England with his wife and three sons. He continued to let his house in north London to the family, and it was here that Elsa and

Ted spent the first years of their marriage. Elsa continued to see her uncle and cousins who all remained in north London when they were adult and had families of their own. The contacts continued even when Elsa and Ted were able to get their own home. They visited the family in Germany as often as they could although Ted was having difficulties in finding employment; a former conscientious objector was often persona non grata and bottom of the pile for job opportunities. Elsa continued to work with her pacifist organisation. Her colleagues had always called her Holly, from her German surname, which she loved - as indeed she loved them all. They gave her not just respect for her origins but self-respect for her identity. Now she was to face the challenge of a marriage of two cultures, much different from just living side by side

Apart from Otto Fricke and the Turck family the others had no thoughts of travelling abroad or going to Germany. They felt that this was the time to hold together and sit tight, ready to make any fresh adjustments which they might have to face. And that was how things were when, finally, the political situation exploded with the assassination of Archduke Ferdinand in Serbia.

CHAPTER TWELVE

PEACE IN THEIR TIME ?

People have said that the first world war was the "war to end all wars". If the war itself had been horrific, many thought that the arrangements consolidated by the Treaty of Versailles would lead to even worse. Not one of the belligerent countries was happy with all aspects. From the signing of the treaty in early 1918, it took many months of discussion - dispute even - and intermediary agreements until the armistice was signed. During that time soldiers continued to be killed and wounded, almost right to the last moment before the ceasefire was declared. Nobody even believed in a satisfactory outcome any more. America, which had come very late into the war, in 1917, wanted more leniency and the Allies seemed almost too exhausted to disagree except for France. The French thought it far too lenient and were particularly unhappy because they had expected to take back the land west of the Rhine - Rhenania. However, the other Allies would not concede this point, and so the French had to be satisfied with recuperating the regions of Alsace-Lorraine. On the back of their dissatisfaction, Clémenceau was defeated in the post-war elections, and his successor Marshall Foch said that it was not a treaty of peace, but an armistice of twenty years. How prophetical this was to be. Finally, the German government hated the Treaty which insisted on Germany admitting total guilt for the war. They were angry at not being included in the peace negotiations, calling it a "Diktat" and a murderous plan.

After hundreds of thousands from all sides had been killed or maimed, in 1919 another catastrophe in the form of a violent epidemic of influenza killed many more. It spread worldwide and was called the "Spanish flu". Those people who had managed to come through all this trauma now had to put their lives back together as best they could. There were those in the surviving younger generations who felt overwhelmed by the sorrow and suffering all around them, and who found escape in the new modern music and dances arriving from America. These usually more well-heeled young people went from one party to another, living to extremes. However, most people looked for work and a fresh start, re-assembling whatever remained of the physical and mental debris.

Carl could be forgiven for never again trusting the politicians and their promises of peace and a better life. He knew of not a single person who had found a happier life or indeed a quiet mind. Once more in their homeland after some forty years in England, Carl and Elise decided not to live in Bad Kreuznach or Kirn. Instead they found a house to rent in a small town called Wesseling, just south of Cologne on the west bank of the Rhine. It was just inside the jurisdiction of the British occupational authorities, and Carl felt safer with them. Also, when the company employing their son-in-law Otto opened premises in Cologne, Carl and Elise were thrilled to have their eldest daughter and her family coming to live in that city. Louise had meanwhile been delivered of a baby daughter who was named Anna-Louise, later to be shortened to Annelie. This last pregnancy had not gone well; Louise had been obliged to spend much time laid up and finally gave birth in hospital. She had been unable to look after her small boys who were put into an orphanage. They did not speak much German at that point and were very resentful of their father whom they blamed for this turbulent new life. When the family finally came together again in Cologne, it was initially in cramped and damp conditions over a fish-shop. Carl and Elise did all they could to help their daughter with the children. In Wesseling they had a garden where the children could run about, where Carl grew fruit and vegetables and Elise kept chickens. But Otto's restless nature once more dominated the lives of the Fricke family, and before long he moved them from one place to another as he amassed one business venture after the other.

Correspondence flowed between Carl and Elise in Wesseling and their children, Elsa and Charlie, who had remained in England. Mail deliveries were unreliable and often disrupted. In early 1923 Carl wrote to Elsa and her husband Ted bemoaning the loss of several letters, which he attributed to the upset caused by "the civilising efforts of our dear neighbours, the French". He said that all railway traffic was disorganised, and all German property was being treated by the French with the contempt they believed it deserved. Carl spoke of their life in Wesseling where he had proudly planted early vegetables and was preparing the soft fruit bushes for the coming season. He worried about Elise who had lost much weight. She had taken on twenty chicks which had grown into laying hens, producing welcome eggs to add to their meagre diet. With their precarious financial situation, Elise would only buy a small amount of butter, margarine, meat or cheese. When the previous year's preserves had run out, the couple ate bread which was tasteless and dry dipped in tea or coffee, if available. So the eggs were a much-needed complement, and they were able to purchase fish fairly economically. Later the chickens could be eaten as well.

Their daughter Maggie was still living with her parents, and her future husband Eric was training with Scholl for some time to come. Louise had been very ill again, her husband Otto was often away travelling and only at home for days at a time. Maggie helped with both households, not always happily but recognising the family needs; she would do so until she could marry Eric and set up their own home. Louise did not have the strength to manage the two older boys, now adolescents and still very unsettled after their tumultuous start in life. They were to be sent to a boarding school either in Rhenania or in the Harz mountain area. Somehow, Louise knew not how,

Otto managed to supply the necessary funds for the costs of medical care for his wife and the education of his children. Louise was also able to get domestic help, and Maggie could return to Wesseling.

In his correspondence with Elsa and Ted in London, Carl wrote of the political and economic conditions in Rhenania. Understandably he had become cynical about the French occupiers. He said that, during the war, much had been made of German "Kultur", and now he was seeing the French "culture". He wrote of their introduction of French civilisation "or should I rather then say syphilisation" in the appearance of "brothels, riding whips, butt ends of rifles, wanton destruction, brutality, sequestrations, suppression of newspapers" and more. Carl told his daughter that, from reading the English newspapers they sent occasionally, he could see that the English people were told only a fraction of what was happening; he expressed the hope that the British would not leave Cologne and the Wesseling area because he feared things would become worse, as they maintained order to a certain extent. He concluded "If the struggle continues much longer, anything may happen". Daughter Elsa and her husband Ted continued to visit Carl and Elise once a year; they were of course warmly welcomed but could see that conditions were taking their toll of the ageing couple.

Allied occupation in Germany finally came to an end and, despite the political manoeuvres of past decades and the questionable settlement of the horrific conflict, people had still managed to come through and re-build some sort of life. Nevertheless, before the mid-1920s Carl had recognised that the galloping inflation, gigantic recession and widespread unemployment were the perfect terrain for the unrest and seizing of power that followed. As the 1920s turned into the early 1930s, and living so close to the vast industrial heartland of Germany, Carl was fearful of yet more upheaval. Louise and her boys were now living in Hamburg where Otto had purchased a big house not far from the Elbe river; Otto was always away on his travels and indeed, from 1926, lived in Ghana for seven years. The boys were in their adolescent and early adult years and, of necessity but perhaps also of inclination, involved in the newly-formed youth movements.

There was a marked difference in the economic and political situations of Germany and Britain, the only similarity being the global depression. Germany had been through years of rampant inflation and political unrest after the war had finished which, in turn, allowed and even encouraged the political developments which were to become a reality, worrying to other nations, as time went by. The German people responded to what they perceived as stronger leadership and fresh ideas favouring the masses of unemployed. As the powers of the new national socialist party, to be called Nazis, grew, so did the confidence and trust of the Germans in their increasing wellbeing, not to say opulence for some. Louise saw her boys grow into tall young men. The eldest Carl became an excellent painter-decorator and had also mastered the skills of marbling and gilding, now becoming much in demand. The younger boys had all completed apprenticeships in business practice and were working in different sectors of commerce. Their young sister Annelie was a lively teenager enjoying the activities in which girls were encouraged, later obliged even, to participate. In 1933 father Otto finally returned from Ghana where he had, supposedly, spent the last seven years. As always he never divulged what he was really doing, just giving his family to understand that he was in the cocoa business. He travelled back via England where he set up several companies purportedly to do with cocoa and asked Ted to watch over these business interests. Ted was not at all enthusiastic to get involved with this; he could not bring himself to trust his brother-in-law who seemed never to give a straight answer to any questions. Otto then went back to Germany and never returned to England thereafter. Some time later Hitler re-introduced conscription to re-build a German army for which he had ambitions. This was quite contrary to the conditions embedded in the Treaty of Versailles and was contested by other nations. However, Hitler ignored all protests from abroad and set about producing the armament he considered best suited to his increasingly powerful military troops. He then sent them in to re-occupy the de-militarised Rhineland, bringing yet another change to the region of Rhenania.

As these events became more frequent and, even before those in Rhenania came about, Elsa and Ted urged Carl and Elise to return and live with them in London, and the old couple were uneasy enough in Germany to accept this offer. The bonus was that they could be near to their other children and grandchildren in England. The welcome by Elsa and Ted could not have been warmer, and Carl and Elise found comfort in the obvious love from their second daughter, now also the proud mother of a little boy. They were also able to visit their youngest daughter Maggie, whose husband was now employed by Scholl in London. Maggie and Eric lived not far away, on the edge of north London, and had a small daughter as well as their son. Son Charlie was trying to revive the essential oil business, but recession and inflation everywhere made this very difficult. His wife Margarethe had occasional work as a journalist, and the couple remained childless. Carl and Elise were rather anxious when Margarethe joined the Christian Science movement.

In 1935 a baby girl was born to Elsa and Ted, and her German grandparents were somehow particularly drawn to the little child. Elise would crawl around on the floor, playing with her latest grandchild to her heart's content. Soon afterwards they also became great-grandparents as Louise's eldest son Carl was now married and had a first son in early 1936; his brother Willi had also married and a small daughter was also born the same year. However, that year also brought grief to Carl and Elise once more when their son Charlie was stricken with a brain haemorrhage. His wife, adhering to her newfound principles of Christian Science, refused all medical intervention, and so Charlie died in much suffering soon after. The family thereafter refused all contact with Margarethe, and she subsequently went to live in South America.

For Carl the worst was to happen in November 1937, when his beloved Elise died very suddenly of heart failure. He was inconsolable and went into a deep depression. Elsa was at a loss to find some way of helping him, and Ted was setting up their own business and needed her help. She did her best for her beloved father but, with two children and a home and husband to look after, she could not find any way of giving him solace. She wrote to his brother, her much loved Uncle Josef, pouring her heart out as she described how her mother Elise had died and how helpless she felt trying to comfort her father. After some time Carl became totally restless and decided to return to Germany to live with his daughter Louise whose sons were now independent, either married or following their professional activities. Only eighteen year old Annelie was still at home. Carl died there in 1940. His brother Josef, now retired, and wife Bertha had returned to Bad Kreuznach where Josef passed away in 1943.

It had not been in Elsa's husband Ted's plans to set up his own business. He had spent the last few years travelling as a salesman for a couple of

German companies mainly connected with the brush trade, and he had not been unhappy with the results. However, after a visit to his German suppliers in late 1936, he became very uneasy about the future. As time went on this feeling did not diminish, and he started looking at his options in the home market. By the time Hitler had annexed Austria and was continuing to further his ambitions for German domination of Europe, Ted had found an opportunity to start making the type of brush for which he already had a home customer base. When the British prime minister Chamberlain announced a peace agreement with Hitler in 1938, like many others Ted was not convinced. The events to follow showed his instinct to be correct.

-0-0-0-0-0-0-0-0-0-0-0-

It was a Sunday morning, warm and sunny - the 3rd September 1939. Ted had gone to work on the nearby allotment he had taken on, with other people in the district, about a year before. The children had gone with him and were happily playing with others, chasing each other up and down the various paths between the plots. Then, halfway through the morning, the bells of the church some way off on the main road began to sound out very strongly. Ted and the other men working on their patches looked up, put their tools to one side and moved toward each other forming a group.

"Well," said Ted. "That's it then. We're at war again".

The men stood together for quite a while, discussing what they thought would be changing. They were of all ages, all had families, and knew that their lives were about to be disrupted again, for the second time in as many decades, again a global war from which even more evil to emerge.

"I can't say that I am happy about being called up, which will surely happen," said one younger man, father of three young children who were happily playing with Ted's daughter. "But I am damned if I want my country to be invaded by that mad man".

"I am over the age for military combat but rest assured, I will be in the civil defence as soon as it gets going. Our homes are precious and, if we all do our bit in whatever way we can, we can stop the blighters".

"Fighting talk, it's good to hear it," said Ted. "You all know my stand in the last war but, this time, I will be the first to defend what we have all worked so hard for. As I'm on the council, I will be in on the organisation of the home guard, so we can get together when I know where we are to set up".

At that point the children, having heard the bells and sensing there was something more than the usual call to church, came running to their dads.

"What's happening?" they all clamoured.

Their fathers looked at each other and realised, more than before, just what was again at stake.

Ted plucked up courage and answered the children. "Look, children. I'm sorry to tell you there is going to be a lot of upset, because the bells meant we have declared war on Germany. But you mustn't be to worried right now because we are going to get organised to make sure nobody takes our country from us. What you can do, and you are good kids already, but you can help especially by doing exactly what you are told when things happen".

The children were silent and did not know what to think. They had heard about the previous war, vaguely because most people did not talk about it; they wanted to put it in the past, and the way they coped was to do just that. But what the children had occasionally picked up was that it was a terrible thing. So it was a subdued group of fathers and children who then made their way back to their homes nearby. As Ted came into his home, being earned with hard work by him and Elsa, seat of his burgeoning business and place of care and safety for parents and children, the aroma of Sunday lunch greeted him. His resolve to defend all of this hardened, and he hoped it would be over more quickly than the last war.

Elsa was in the kitchen cooking, a job which she loved and which she was very good at. Tears were in her eyes and Ted saw immediately that she had been crying. He saw she had heard the church bells and knew what it meant. He knew she was torn once again but he also knew her heart belonged to him and her family in England, and that it was her love for her sister in Germany that was hurting her.

Peace was apparently beyond the high price already paid, and another generation faced the horrors of conflict both at home and abroad. Once more there was heart break for Elsa in Britain and sister Louise in Germany as it became obvious that, this time, the members of both sides of the family would have to join in the conflict in one way or another. All Louise's sons - Elsa's nephews - were conscripted. The eldest Carl went one step further by becoming a member of the Waffen SS. The others went into the Wehrmacht. Otto Fricke was beyond the age of conscription but, in his usual secretive maverick way, he was involved in the Nazi movement and his knowledge of Britain and British commerce had its value. He proclaimed in post-war years that, had Germany been victorious, he was earmarked to become mayor of the city of Birmingham. Louise's daughter Annelie was married at the young age of twenty-one to an officer of the Wehrmacht. There could be no doubt of their involvement, and Louise did the only thing she could: ignore the politics and concentrate on the growing family. Carl had four children, and Willi two. The family was based in Hamburg.

Elsa was more intensely affected by the situation. Although British born and married to an Englishman, she was again in essence an enemy alien in Britain and was, in fact, registered with the police to that effect. She was once more in mental turmoil; she felt herself to be British through and through, but she could not bring herself to deny her German family and heritage. However, she knew it had to be put aside for the time being, and so she concentrated on helping with the family business and looking after the family as best she could. Although she had sometimes felt unhappy about waiting so long to conceive, she was now glad her children were too young to be involved in the fighting. The constant bombing alone did not let her forget her mental agony. Of necessity all contact with her sister Louise had ceased in 1940, with the last communication allowed being the news of her father's death. Thereafter it was to be more than five years before there was any chance of re-establishing contact. Although Elsa did not learn of her uncle Josef's death until after the war, she was glad that her parents were no longer there to witness yet more tragedy.

The war continued month after month, year after year, with ever more devastating effect on both sides. The development of increasingly powerful military equipment and weapons brought destruction to towns and cities all over Britain and Europe, not to mention the middle and far east.

Civilians were no longer safe. Indeed they were killed by the hundreds as targets moved from one industrial area to another, or when bombing was carried out callously to demoralise or in so-called retaliation. Hatred for the Nazis intensified, and people again blamed the Germans for this renewed horrendous conflict. Even Ted identified with this and let it be known that he would not have been a conscientious objector this second time round. Although it was not aimed at her, Elsa felt terrible and somehow guilty although reproach was never laid at her door. She could not understand her emotions and suffered from intermittent depression, which she hid behind her busy daily activities. She was glad and relieved each day when the children came safely home from school; she was glad and relieved when her husband came back safely from his business activities, which sometimes involved travelling to other cities, and from his fire-watching duties in the home guard service; she was glad and relieved when yet another day passed without their home suffering from more than blast damage to the taped-up windows. But what Elsa found almost impossible to bear was the relentless bombing with ever more terrifying new weapons, and the knowledge that her beloved sister would be living with the same daily worries.

When Hitler's Germany had developed the V1 pilotless bombs and sent these over to the south-east of England and London from launchpads in France, Belgium and Holland, even the children - hitherto resilient and adaptable - were petrified.

Elsa and Ted had kept their children with them in London up to that point, not wanting them to be subjected to the trauma of separation and homesickness. Now they decided to evacuate them and found places for them in far away Yorkshire. Their son, at fourteen, was sent to live on a farm and in fact found country life much to his taste. Their eight-year old little girl was placed with an old lady; the child did indeed suffer from homesickness. When she ran away after a month, they decided to bring her home where, if her young life was always disrupted, at least she would not be lonely. After the so-called buzz-bombs or doodlebugs came the V2 rockets which were even more destructive but which, on the whole, people found easier to cope with. The psychological effect of the V1 which could be seen and heard at close quarters just before it fell to earth was felt by many to be far more intense than the V2s which did not announce their arrival, simply exploded on impact. If people heard the explosion, they knew they were lucky enough to be safe, at least that time around.

At last, at long last, the war was brought to an end in Europe as the allied troops recovered one country after another, and pushed into Germany from all sides until meeting in Berlin. The destruction was on a scale never seen before but worse was coming to light. The unimaginable horror of the concentration camps and gas chambers, and the wretchedness of the people who had managed to survive, was opened up by allied troops. For many of them it was worse than anything they had experienced before. The only thing that could be said was that the enormous effort to crush the Nazi regime was more than justified, in a way that had never been conceived. All that remained for the Allies was to now conquer the Japanese. There were horrors to be found in the far east as well, and the final horror of all was the dropping of two atom bombs on Nagasaki and Hiroshima. It was as if there could be no end to new forms of the atrocity of war. The whole of humanity was battered and bruised.

CHAPTER THIRTEEN

1948 : THE REUNION

Once the postal service for civilian communication had been re-established between Britain and Germany, the two sisters sought to find each other again. Elsa had written to the last address she had for Louise but had received no response, and she feared the worst. She was setting about making enquiries through the Red Cross when a letter came with other post distinguishing itself by its foreign stamp. However, the writing was familiar - Louise had written her first post-war letter to her sister's address, firstly hoping that the house was still standing and secondly that her sister and family were still living there.

Elsa had picked up the small pile of letters, most of which were in connection with the family business. Immediately she noticed the different envelope and instinctively knew what it was. Her emotion was such that she sat down suddenly and could not move. Ted came in and saw her.

"Elsa, you are white as a sheet. What is the matter?"

Elsa held out the bunch of letters, and Ted also immediately saw what had happened.

"It's from Louise. It's what you have been waiting for. Oh Elsa, don't cry, my dear. Look, it's her handwriting, so she is still alive. She has come through".

Elsa sat there for a long time, just looking at the envelope in her hand. She was overjoyed but, at the same time, was fearful of what news the letter might contain. Finally she became calmer and opened the envelope. There was just a single page inside, written on exercise book paper. On it Louise said, very simply, that she hoped Elsa and her family were still at this address. If they were not, she asked whoever had opened the letter to either forward it to them, if their address was known or, please, to send her a brief reply to say their whereabouts were unknown. Louise expressed the hope that her fears of their absence would be wrong, and that they had survived as well as possible. She concluded that she would write no more this time but, if her prayers were answered and Elsa replied, she would welcome news of her English relatives and then send news of them all in Germany.

Elsa abandoned all housework and office work, and sat down to write a long letter to her much loved sister. She began by expressing the wish that they had all come through and this, hopefully, without serious consequences. She had so many questions but told her sister she would not plague her with them at this stage. Then she passed on to writing about her own family and how things were now, in the post-war times when everyone was still in the throes of picking up the threads of their lives. Elsa told Louise she was going to pass on the good news to their younger sister Maggie who would also be happy to know that contact had been re-established.

During the following months, which became years, the sisters wrote as often as they could. Whilst the English families had come through at least physically intact and with their homes still in one piece, despite the continued severe rationing of food and clothing, not to mention heating materials such as coke or coal, they were fairly confident that their lives would gradually improve and their children had a brighter future. For Louise and her family, on the other hand, their existence was not as simple. Firstly, two of the Fricke boys had lost their lives in the conflict, or at least it was certain that one of them had. The youngest son Otto had been killed in an air raid; the second son Paul had been taken prisoner by the Russians and was known to have been put in a Russian camp for German prisoners of war. Louise harboured hope against hope that he would return because they had never received definite confirmation of his death. She was glued to the radio when, periodically, lists were read out of German prisoners freed to return home. Paul Fricke was never among those names. Eldest son Carl had also been on the Russian front but had managed to escape being made a prisoner. He had walked hundreds of miles back to Hamburg where his young family, now with four children, were still in their own home; miraculously this was still undamaged despite its situation near to the river Elbe and docks. Louise's daughter Annelie and her family were living with brother Carl; her husband had lost a leg and was coping as best he could with a basic wooden limb; they had their little boy but so far no further children. They were intending to find some land and build their own house.

Both Louise and Otto and son Willi's family had been bombed out of their separate homes and were now living together. No-one had known of Willi's whereabouts at the end of the war until, one day, his wife was passing the ruins of their former home and saw smoke rising. Thinking it strange she went in, picking her way through, and saw what she thought to be a tramp crouched in the corner by a meagre fire of wood taken from the debris. When she spoke gently to the man - there were so many lost souls - she saw that it was Willi. When he did not answer her but just looked blankly, she told him to stay where he was. Returning swiftly home, she told her mother-in-law Louise what had happened, and the two women hurried back to the ruins. Between them they managed to get him up and took him to where they were all living. Willi had been wounded in the head, and they could see the scar badly healed over. He had no memory of where he had been and hardly recognised his family, although he seemed to accept who they were. Later on, when they got him to hospital, after several examinations they were told the shrapnel was still lodged in his brain but that it was too dangerous to remove it. They would never learn what had happened to him.

As time went by and the sisters' relationship became, if anything, deeper than before, Elsa determined to find a way of bringing Louise to England for a break, if not exactly a holiday, from the immensely sad situation in which she lived. With all that emerged from the aftermath of the Nazi regime and the Nuremberg trials, nobody could truly explain or understand what had happened. Although in certain circles there were moves toward helping Germany to re-establish itself, such as American aid programmes (largely politically motivated) but also religiously-based self-help assisted programmes in the mining areas, the German people were anything but settled with zones controlled by Russia, Britain, America and France. It was fortunate for Elsa that Louise lived in the British zone, which made all the steps she needed to take a lot simpler. She finally obtained permission for the visit, and Ted offered to pay for the air fare. Louise was more than appreciative of this gesture from her brother-in-law because it removed the need for an arduous journey by rail and sea. It took some while for her to obtain a passport, paid for by her children clubbing together, and the necessary visa; however, her entitlement to British nationality also played a very helpful part in gaining the agreement of the British authorities.

In 1948, after more than a decade of separation, the sisters finally came together again. Determined to make the journey as comfortable and quick as possible, Elsa splashed out on the services of a chauffeur-driven car to pick up her sister from the airport of Northolt, to the west of London. She stood watching the arrival and saw the passengers coming off the plane. At first she thought her sister could not be among them and panic started to set in, until she realised with a shock that a thin elderly lady with white hair was actually her beloved Louise. Then she was grateful for the time it took for Louise to come through the passport and customs barriers; she did not want her sister to see her disarray at the obvious toll taken by time and events. Elsa suddenly asked herself whether she had also changed to such an extent but she need not have worried. Louise came through, carrying a small case, and saw Elsa. The two women embraced warmly, not wanting to let go of each other. They did not talk very much on the car journey home, just held hands and absorbed the moment. It was the first time that Louise had seen her sister's home, although she had heard much about it. Her brother-in-law Ted opened the front door to welcome her and also embraced her warmly. He had always cared a great deal about Louise, although he could not bring himself to like her husband Otto.

For the next three weeks Louise and Elsa spent hours talking, sometimes with difficulty when it came to the war years and pre-war years even. They were joined once or twice by sister Maggie who, as always, was difficult to read; she had never revealed her feelings much. It seemed that she was pleased to see her eldest sister but somehow the warmth did not come through.

Louise also got to know the younger generation, a nephew and niece in both families, of ages ranging from twenty-two to thirteen years. Elsa's son Paul had gone into farming, so was no longer at home, but her daughter was a teenager at grammar school. Louise developed a friendly relationship with the girl who was more akin to her own eldest grandchildren, thus cousins once removed. As the days went by Elsa and Louise both put the past firmly behind, thinking that the best - indeed the only - way forward was to encourage the adolescents to write to each other. In this way the sisters hoped that both sides of the family would become acquainted and learn to appreciate the cultural differences.

In the years following this visit Elsa and Louise continued their correspondence and worked hard on arranging visits. The first to take place, in 1951, was that of Elsa and her son Paul to the families in Hamburg. It was in celebration of Paul's 21st birthday and, as he was now in agriculture, of necessity a winter visit. This was followed in the early summer of the same year by a visit arranged for Louise's two eldest grandchildren, Gerd who was Carl's son and Christa who was Willi's daughter. Louise had some misgivings about Gerd who was of a very nervous disposition; he had been badly traumatised by the war and, at nearly 16, had occasional bed-wetting accidents. Elsa protested that this was unimportant and, indeed, from the moment of this visit on Gerd never had another such incident. On some days the two youngsters were able to go to school with Elsa's daughter Ruth and seemed otherwise to enjoy their time in England. When it was time for them to return to Germany, Ruth went with them and met all the families there. This went so well that, on finishing grammar school a year later, Ruth went to Hamburg for a year to continue her studies at a very good language and business school. During that time she came to learn much about her German roots and the culture in general, which was greatly different from anything she knew before.

Ruth had a particularly good relationship with Louise's daughter Annelie and her family. Annelie and her husband had acquired a plot of land and were building their own house. Despite being handicapped with an artificial leg, husband Richard was a travelling salesman; he had a specially adapted car and was away for days at a time on business. A second child had arrived to complete the family, now a toddler they called Heidi. Because the couple had so little leisure time together, one day Ruth offered to baby-sit the two children whenever they felt like an evening out. Their young son Peter was a lively intelligent child, now ten years old, who loved nothing better than to spend the evening playing mikado with Ruth. Despite their difference in age, the two cousins became close over the years.

Gradually the lives of all the families, both in Germany and in England, became more peaceful and comfortable. The younger generation on both sides were all working hard to make good homes for their own children. Visits between the two countries by the cousins were infrequent during those years, none of them having a lot of spare time for such activities. The sisters wrote to each other at least once or twice a month, and Elsa went to Hamburg in 1960 to attend the golden wedding celebration of Louise and Otto. However, they were of the generation which was getting old and fragile. Indeed, Otto died in 1965 and Louise followed him six years later in 1971. Elsa's Ted passed away in 1976, and sister Maggie in 1977 - the latter's husband Eric had in fact been the first to go in 1958. Elsa herself lived to the age of almost 93, passing away in 1987. However, the sisters' wishes were granted: there was regular contact between Peter and Ruth, if possible visits with their spouses and maybe an offspring or two, and in between conversations over the telephone. So the families had survived the rifts inflicted on them by so many leaders, both political and military, to share joyful times whenever possible.

-0-0-0-0-0-0-0-0-0-0-0-

One evening in 1991 the telephone rang in Ruth's home.

"2315, good evening".

"Hello Ruth, it's Peter. How are you?"

"Peter, how lovely to hear from you. We are all fine. You must be psychic because I was just thinking of you. But how are you all doing?"

"Busy as ever, but everyone is well and happy - so far so good, as they say. Except perhaps my mum".

"Oh Peter, I'm sorry to hear that. Is it her heart again? What a good thing that she is living in your house, so you can be at her side straight away".

"No, her heart is not the problem this time, although the bad circulatory problems don't help. I think it's more her mental health. She went off the other day, on her own, which is quite normal. She lives independently in the flat above ours, so we wouldn't normally worry. But a neighbour found her wandering round the town as if she were lost, and she didn't seem to know why she was there. We went to get her, just as if we were meeting her anyway, and brought her home and she has been fine ever since. But we shall have to keep an eye on her, as discreetly as we can".

The two cousins continued to exchange news about various other members of the family, and then Peter changed the subject.

"Ruth, you remember we had a long chat when you were last here about the various documents and photos we both have of many of our venerable ancestors?"

"Of course. I have the stories put together by our ancestor Josef, my great-uncle and your great-great-uncle! They are a bit higgledy-piggledy, and in German script. But I learnt how to read that, and so I thought that I would translate the texts into English, and then later try to put them into some sort of historical order. I know you are thinking 'why English' but, although my German is good, it is not that good!".

"Well, listen. I have to go to Scotland on business in two weeks' time, so why don't I add on a couple of days to see you, and I'll bring some photos and papers I have. We could go through things together, you can take copies of whatever you don't already have, and we can share our memories of different events as well".

"Peter, that would be so good. Let me know the dates and I'll make sure I don't do anything else then. Meanwhile my greetings to your wife and children, and love to my lovely cousin Annelie. I am so sorry she is poorly, and do hope it is a temporary hiccup only. Sometimes old people have little episodes like that, and then they are fine again. So let's hope it is one of those".

Peter and Ruth exchanged more such visits periodically over the coming years. In this manner a considerable collection of written memories, letters and pictures came about. It became obvious that this was an exceptional opportunity to assemble them in better chronological order, and present them to the younger members of the family. A first narrative was written which covered the emigration of the various members of the family from Germany to England. It contained many photographs and copies of the original texts in some cases. However, the narratives collected by Josef Holzbacher preceded that period by some one hundred years. It had to be worthwhile to write them in the form of a book, the first narratives as chronicles to be followed by how those who emigrated to Britain spent their lives. To make this relevant to the lives of the latest generation, it would show how - century after century, decade after decade - ordinary families are affected by the ambitions and manipulations of the leaders of nations whoever they may be. It was also thought that a little imaginative dialogue and setting a scene to match would help to link the various narratives and make their reading come alive.

So let us hope that Josef and Illa and Valentine, the main historians whose enthusiasm provided such rich pickings, would be thrilled and proud of the descendants who appreciated their efforts.

People's hopes are always invested in their children and grandchildren. When they are burdened with cataclysmic events, especially those whose effects are long-lasting, can it be reasonable to still believe those hopes might one day be realised?

In 1984, Elsa had reached her 90th birthday. She was the only person left of her generation and lived with her daughter and family in a town just north of London. All the relatives and friends were asked to a sort of open day at their home, whereby those who could make it would be able to spend whatever time they liked with the kind and caring lady who had been part of their lives. Among them were her niece Annelie and her nephew Carl, who had come especially from Germany. Her sister Maggie's children, son Alan and daughter Jessie, also came from their homes in the east of England. This was an occasion where some of the German relatives could meet, perhaps for the first time, the descendants of Carl and Elise who had made their lives in England. Tired though she was after this exciting day, Elsa was deeply moved by the effort made by all her guests not just to celebrate her nine decades but also to show that, no matter what, the family ties still survived. Her thoughts turned to her parents and to her sister Louise, and she imagined how

pleased they would have been, how they would rejoice and be healed.

Some years later Annelie and her son Peter decided to celebrate the family ties which had been so tested during the 20th century. On that July day they welcomed all those descendants who were able to come to the gathering held in the courtyard of Peter's family house in southern Germany. In relation to Carl and Elise there were 6 of the 9 grandchildren, 6 of the 17 great-grandchildren, and 4 of the 21 great-great-grandchildren, making 16 descendants. Accompanying them were spouses and other relatives by marriage, making a party of 31 persons in all.

What better illustration could there be of the resilience of the human spirit?

ACKNOWLEDGEMENTS

Robin Scutarius is a pen-name because the writer/presenter of the stories would have had nothing to relate, were it not for the diligence of Josef and Louise in particular. Without their care in preserving letters, cards, newspaper cuttings and so much more, there would have been no message to pass on.

Peter was unfortunately struck by terminal cancer when he was only 69 years old. He cared a great deal about his ancestral family, and also felt a very strong connection to the part of the family which had remained in England. Therefore, it was essential that his cousin Ruth should carry the torch, and that is how this book came into being.

For assistance in how to bring the book to published fruition, thanks must go to Ruth's son Gerard. Without his "on-line" technical assistance, it might still be only the contents of a desktop file.

Printed in Poland
by Amazon Fulfillment
Poland Sp. z o.o., Wrocław